D1740682

The Indian Subcontinent
India, Pakistan and Bangladesh

Nicholas Pinfield

AHMED IQBAL ULLAH
RACE RELATIONS
ARCHIVE
MANCHESTER

Longman
London and New York

Longman Group UK Limited
*Longman House, Burnt Mill, Harlow, Essex, CM20 2JE, England
and Associated Companies throughout the World.*
Published in the United States of America
by Longman Inc., New York
© Longman Group UK Limited 1991

*All rights reserved. No part of this publication may be
reproduced, stored in a retrieval system, or transmitted in
any form or by any means, electronic, mechanical,
photocopying, recording, or otherwise, without either the
prior written permission of the Publishers or a licence
permitting restricted copying issued by the Copyright
Licensing Agency Ltd, 90 Tottenham Court Road, London W1P 9HE.*

First published 1991
Second impression 1994
ISBN 0 582 20661 8

Set in 11/12 pt Baskerville Roman Linotron
Produced by Longman Singapore Publishers Pte Ltd
Printed in Singapore

Library of Congress Cataloging-in-Publication Data

Pinfield, Nicholas.
    The Indian subcontinent : India, Pakistan, and Bangladesh /
Nicholas Pinfield.
        p.   cm. — (Modern times)
    Includes index.
    Summary: Discusses the history of India, Pakistan, and Bangladesh
with emphasis on the role of nationalism and the influence of the
long British presence in the region.
        ISBN 0–582–20661–8
        1. South Asia — History — Juvenile literature. [1. South Asia —
History.]   I. Title.   II. Series: Modern times (Harlow, England)
    DS340.P56   1991
    954 — dc20   90-26449
                                                                                         CIP
                                                                                          AC

British Library Cataloguing in Publication Data

Pinfield, Nicholas
    The Indian subcontinent : India, Pakistan and Bangladesh.
    — (Modern times).
    1. South Asia, history
    I. Title   II. Series
    954
    ISBN 0–582–20661–8

Contents

Introduction

India is a great ragged triangle jutting southward from the land mass of Asia into the Indian Ocean. In the north the mighty Himalayas – the rooftop of the world – form one main region of the subcontinent of India. A second region lies to the south of the mountains, in the rich and fertile plains of the rivers fed by Himalayan snows, especially the Indus in the west and the Ganges in the east. To the south of the plains is a high central plateau which stretches a thousand miles towards the southern point of the triangle at Cape Comorin. This third region is known as the Deccan, the South.

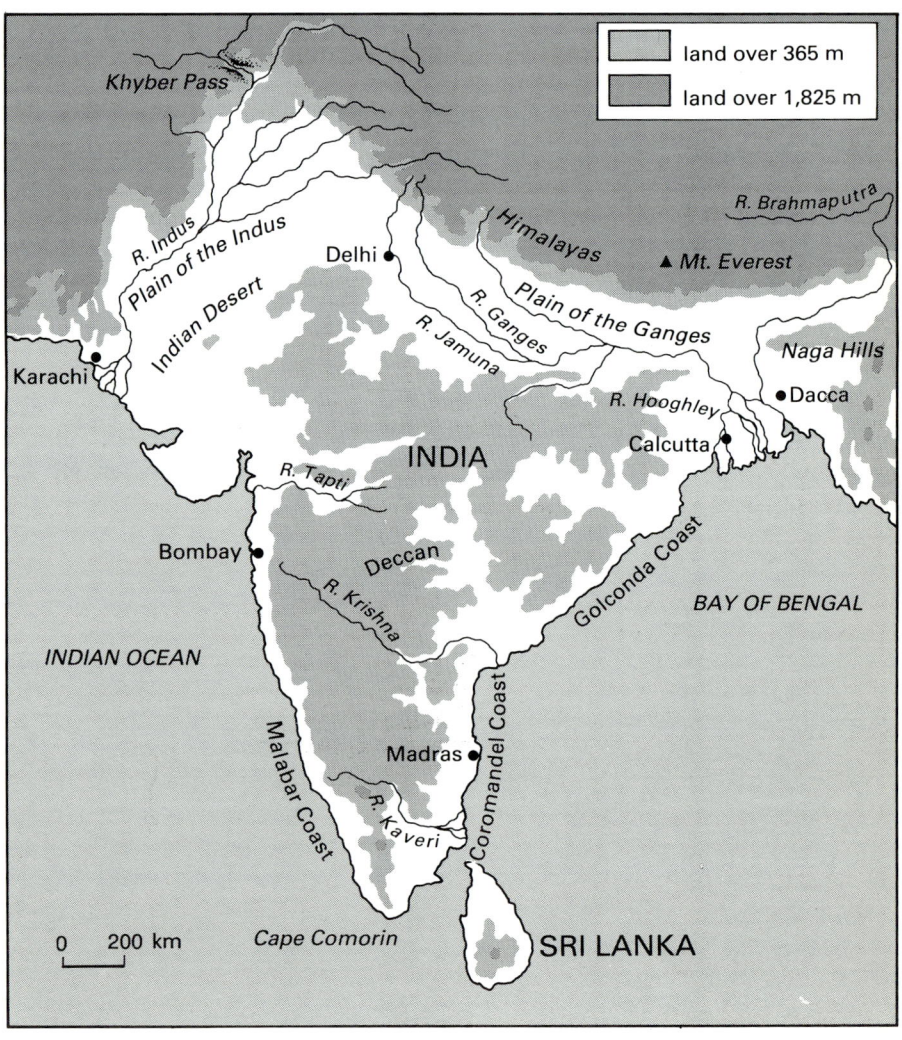

Geographical features of the Indian subcontinent.

PART ONE

INDIA AND POLITICAL RULE

1
The Great Indian Peninsula

About half-way between the great port cities of Bombay and Calcutta is the town of Dongargarh. In the middle of the nineteenth century it was a small village with perhaps twenty houses. It is at the centre of an agricultural area, for the light sandy soil of the surrounding plains is fertile. Local farmers could easily grow more wheat than they needed for themselves.

Railways and their effects

In 1853, 600 miles away to the west the first few miles of railway track in India were opened in Bombay. This was one of the lines which were to be built to link the main cities of India. By 1871 a branch of the Great Indian Peninsula Railway passed through Dongargarh, going on to join the Madras Railway at Raipur, 100 miles down the line.

A few years before, an enterprising trading firm from nearby Nagpur (see map, page 9) sent their agent to settle in Dongargarh. They knew that the railway was coming and wanted to profit from it.

The agent began to buy grain at the weekly market. Word got around. Soon farmers from the fertile plains around came to the market to sell. More traders came from Nagpur and more farmers from surrounding districts. The railway brought a ready market for the grain of the plains.

Across Central India, 1885

By 1885 Dongargarh had grown to a small town, with perhaps 2,000 houses. In the busy time after the harvest, an estimated 100,000 thronged the daily market. Into this bustle of people, carts and bullocks, plunged merchants looking for bargains. Many came hundreds of miles by train, some from as far away as Bombay.

Returning to Bombay by train was a long, hot and uncomfortable journey which might take two days if there were no breakdowns or other delays. Many travellers would be merchants. Some might be wealthy men, but in the traditional Hindu social system of caste they had lower status than the priests (Brahmins) and warriors (Kshatrias) (see page

11). Some merchants were not Hindus at all. The Parsi community from Bombay and its area were particularly successful in trade. Originally from Persia (Iran) they had settled on India's west coast and had kept their own traditions alive.

In December 1885 merchants made up one important group of travellers steaming west towards the big junction at Bhusawal. Here the train stopped for a while. It was joined by lawyers and doctors, amongst others, who were on their way from Allahabad in Central Provinces to take part in the first meeting of an organisation called the Indian National Congress, to be held in Bombay.

Mile after mile of the plains of central India slipped by. They were crossing a plateau and the first big river they passed flowed south then east, but before Akola the rivers began to flow to the west. Almost everyone in these parts worked on the land, men, women and children. Life was hard and although there were some wealthier farmers, the great majority were greatly in debt to local money lenders. The poorest might well lose their small plots of land and join the desperate army of landless peasants.

Famines

In good years when the rains came on time, such people could just about survive. The relentless work in the fields and a poor diet took their toll and diseases like cholera and smallpox claimed many lives. Less than ten years before, in the summer of 1876, the rains failed in the whole of central and southern India. The entire crop of grain withered and died. There were no reserves because the previous year had also been a bad one. Later, some Indians argued that the British did not pay enough attention to building up such reserves for bad years. The desperate situation became even worse when the summer south-west monsoon rains failed again in 1877.

Nobody will ever know exactly how many died as a result of starvation and disease in those terrible famine years. The best estimate is that over 5 million died in India as a direct result of the famine, out of a population of about 200 million.

The Nagpur area had, in fact, escaped the worst of the famine. Grain from the area had been sent by rail and sea south to the most affected parts. In 1878 the summer rains did come to the south, bringing an end to the famine. Now, seven years later, the merchants were on a train again, carrying grain out of the area – but this time it was bound for Bombay and export.

The line had been running west along the valley of the Tapti River, with mountains climbing high to the north and south. At Bhusawal the line joined the main Bombay-Calcutta route and swung south-west into the hills. After Deolali the line began the steep, winding descent down the hills, the Western Ghats, to the coastal plain and the city of Bombay.

The line twisted around the shoulders of the rocky mountains, sometimes on narrow ledges over a precipice, sometimes tunnelling through the rock mass. The railway engineers and their gangs had to drive their lines through some of the most difficult country in the

Hyderabad station in 1889.

world, from dry deserts to delta marshlands, from dense jungles to soaring mountains.

Many of the Indians travelling to the Bombay meeting were the sort of men who might have asked whether this effort and money should not have been spent on canals rather than railways. Railways were a means of transport but canals gave both a means of irrigating the fields and moving the crops to market.

Bombay, 1885

The line ended in Bombay. Here was a very different face of India. This island city was home for at least 800,000 people and growing fast. By far the largest on India's west coast it was, with Calcutta away to the north-east, India's busiest port. Just over twenty years before, the original seven small islands had been joined together and a major building boom started.

Railways have been described as a means of spearheading an attack on traditional ways of existence. A hundred years before, Indian spinners and weavers had produced by far the largest amount of cotton cloth in the world. Now they had been overtaken by the factories in Lancashire, and British steamships and railways brought Manchester goods to the bazaars in every town and village in India.

The wealth of the city could be seen in the fine public buildings and the head offices of trading companies and banks. Many ships loaded and unloaded their cargoes in the busy docks. Passenger ships arrived here too. For many visitors, Bombay was their first experience of India.

Off the main streets and away from the grand buildings was a very different city. In cramped and insanitary conditions most of Bombay's inhabitants struggled to make some sort of living. Disease was rife. Infant mortality was high and life expectancy low. The city's population kept increasing, though, swelled by desperate people from the surrounding region of Maharashtra in search of work.

2
India in the nineteenth century

The first Europeans to establish trading links with India were from Portugal. They arrived at the start of the sixteenth century. They set up their main base in 1510 at a place called Goa on the west coast of India.

For a hundred years the Portuguese had no serious rivals in the trade from India to Europe. Each year their fleet of ships loaded with pepper and other valuable spices made the long journey from Goa to Lisbon.

Early in the seventeenth century merchants from other European countries arrived on the coast of India. Trading companies were set up by the Dutch, English, French and Danish. They built trading posts, called factories, mostly along India's east coast. They were all there for the same reason. Huge profits could be made by shipping textiles, sugar, indigo and saltpetre back to Europe.

The Mughal Empire

By 1700 the Mughal Empire covered the whole of India except the southernmost tip. From his palace in Delhi, the Emperor Aurangzeb now ruled by far the greatest empire India had ever seen.

Successful trading flourishes under strong and stable government. There had been great civilisations and strong rulers in India for at least 4,000 years. None of these rulers ever seemed likely to control more than a part of India until one of Aurangzeb's ancestors invaded India from the north-west in 1523.

Muslim invaders These invaders from Central Asia were Muslims and known as Mughals. They established a Mughal Empire which controlled most of India by the time of Emperor Akbar the Great, who ruled roughly at the time of Elizabeth I in England. The language at court was Persian. So, too, were the styles of art and architecture. Even so, the Mughals

The old Mosque in Delhi, the capital of the Mughal Empire. The Mosque shows clearly the Persian influence on Mughal architecture.

respected the Hindu religion of the local people. The strength of the Empire depended on Hindu Princes who served the Mughals as local rulers, upholding laws and collecting taxes.

Mughal power and the peace of the Mughal Empire were not to last. The Empire was weakening because of struggles within its ruling family. Emperors of the eighteenth century were not as successful as Akbar and Aurangzeb in insisting on loyalty from local rulers. Some of these began to act as if they were independent Princes.

Threats

The Mughal weakness offered a real opportunity for others to seize power. There were two main threats to Mughal control. One was from the Maratha Confederacy, an independent Hindu state on India's west coast. This loose grouping of powerful chiefs had built up their armies and, in little more than fifty years, had come to control a huge area of north and central India.

Just outside India to the north-west is Afghanistan (see map, page 9). This is the traditional invasion route into India, and the second threat to the Mughals.

Marathas and Afghans

Around 1705 Ahmad Shah, the ruler of Afghanistan, began to move his armies in strength into India. In 1756 he captured Delhi, still the capital of the Mughal Empire. The Maratha army moved to challenge the Afghans but at the battle of Panipat in 1761 they were heavily defeated. The Marathas were not seen as far north as Delhi for a decade. But the Afghan ruler did no better. His troops mutinied. Ahmad Shah had to return to Afghanistan. He never came back.

In fact the power vacuum left by the collapse of the Mughal Empire was filled by a quite different group of people. Their bases were scattered along the coast. They had only a tiny army but it was well trained and supplied by sea. They were not a powerful state or a confederacy. They were not even Indian. They were members of a European trading company and their main aim was profit.

European rivalry

The Mughal Emperors had encouraged trade with other countries. Europe was a good market for Indian goods, especially cotton cloth, and the rulers had made the various European trading companies welcome. With trade, cash for buying and selling became more important than bartering or exchanging goods without money. Local Princes and the Mughals began to demand that peasant farmers paid their taxes in cash rather than crops or products.

East India companies

The companies were rivals in trade but there were good profits for all so long as there was peace and stability in India. 'The United Company of Merchants of England trading to the East Indies', known as 'The East India Company', was one of the strongest. Established by a charter of Queen Elizabeth in 1600, it was forty or so years older than its main rival, the French East India Company.

Robert Clive

As Mughal power tottered in the middle of the eighteenth century a race began between the companies for political power and wealth. At the same time Britain and France were at war in Europe. The governments of France and Britain sent money, supplies and troops and India became a part of the battleground.

Neither the French nor the British had many troops but they hired local soldiers. Robert Clive out-fought the opposing French general, Joseph Dupleix. It was clear by the mid-1760s that the British East India Company had come out on top. Not only had they seen off the challenge of the French and other companies, but their advanced military technology had no rival anywhere in India. The East India Company came to control large areas of India, especially in the southeast and in Bengal. In England their charter said that they were the only English company allowed to trade with India. This monopoly of trade made sure that their supply of cotton goods was protected, but greed drove them much further. In 1765 the Mughal Emperor gave the East India Company the right to receive taxes from the whole of

Bengal in exchange for propping up his weakening empire. The merchants had, in effect, become rulers of key regions of India.

The spread of British power

By the start of the nineteenth century the East India Company ruled even larger areas of India. As traders, their main bases were port cities: Calcutta in the north-east, Madras in the south-east and Bombay in the west. More and more goods flowed through these ports. The taxes could now help to buy Indian goods for export to Britain. Large profits were made by the members of the Company in London.

Traders in India

Other commercial and business interests in Britain wanted a share of these profits. After a long campaign they managed to have the East India Company's monopoly of trade with India ended in 1833. These businessmen invested money in railway companies which began to build the railway system in India from the early 1850s.

Some Indians welcomed the British when they first arrived, especially if their area had suffered disorder with the collapse of Mughal rule. The Mughals had prepared the ground in many ways for a strong, central government in India with a reasonably efficient system of taxation and local government. The same families which had done well serving the Mughal Emperors in Delhi were quite prepared to do the same for the new British rulers.

Wars of conquest

Other Indians were not going to accept the British without a fight. The Maratha Confederacy was only finally defeated after a series of three wars ending in 1823. The Sikh kingdom of Punjab was only conquered in 1849. The mainly Muslim kingdom of Oudh in the north was under direct British rule by 1856. There was no fighting but simmering discontent.

For almost all Indians, the changes that came with developing British rule were unsettling. The rulers spoke a new language, English, and expected those Indians who worked for them to speak it too. There were new types of schools, there were many missionaries and new Christian churches. There were trains and the electric telegraph. Many of these challenged traditional Indian customs in a way that the Mughals had never done.

Rebellion, 1857

There were good reasons why many Indians felt oppressed by having to live according to British (and Christian) traditions and views of law and morality. In 1857 these deep-rooted discontents were ignited when one section of the Indian people took violent action to protect their customs. Their discontent had found a focus. The Company had many Indian soldiers, or Sepoys, in its armies in north India. Some of these troops accepted that they were treated differently from white soldiers; others resented this. The resentment flared into open rebellion when the troops in north India were issued with a new rifle. Its cartridges were said to be greased with a mixture of beef and pork fat, which made them offensive to both Hindus and Muslims. They had to be bitten before they could be used. Whole regiments of Indian troops rebelled, killing their British officers and often their families.

Most of the Company's troops in other parts of India did not support the rebels, yet rebellion did spread in northern and central India to some Princes, landowners and peasants who united in their opposition to foreign rule. It was put down by troops loyal to the Company but only after fourteen months of bitter fighting, with atrocities on both sides. In 1858, almost as soon as the rebellion was crushed, the British government abolished the powers of the East India Company. The British part of India was now ruled directly by the government in London.

The structure of government

The British government minister responsible for Indian affairs was the Secretary of State for India. This was an important political job and the Secretary changed quite frequently, either because the British Prime Minister moved his ministers around or because the government itself was voted out of office.

Government in India

Because the Secretary of State was based in London, many thousands of slow miles away, the government appointed a person living in India to have the full authority of the government. At first he was called the Governor General; later, in 1868, he became the Viceroy. The change took place because the British Parliament had declared that Queen Victoria was Empress of India.

The really important decisions in India were taken at weekly meetings of the Executive Council. This group was made up of the Viceroy, the Commander-in-Chief of the Army in India and five senior government officials. The meetings were held in private and all the members were British.

A larger group called the Legislative Council also usually met once a week but the public could attend and listen. Its task was to discuss the laws in force in India, suggest changes to existing ones or put forward new laws entirely. It was made up of the members of the Executive Council, together with an extra group of government officials and a group of between ten and sixteen non-officials representing Indian and European sections of society. Non-officials were people who did not hold government jobs. Most were prominent in trade and industry and a few of them were Indian, not European. They were the only Indians who could take part in making the major decisions which could affect the lives of Indians throughout the subcontinent.

Calcutta the capital was itself in the area called Bengal in the northeast of India (see the map opposite). It was one of the three main blocks of India ruled directly by the British. The official in charge in Bengal was the Lieutenant Governor. The two other main blocks,

Bombay in the west and Madras in the south, had Governors in charge. Bengal, Bombay and Madras had their own Provincial Legislative Councils. These Provincial Councils only discussed things to do with their own regions and their decisions had to be agreed by the Viceroy. A few Indians could serve on these Councils.

In 1885 Punjab and the North Western Provinces still did not have Legislative Councils. Other areas, for example, Burma and the Central Provinces, came under the direct control of the Viceroy.

The extent of British power c.1900.

Districts

Throughout those parts of India ruled by the British the basic unit of administration was the District. It was controlled by the District Officer, often called the Collector-Magistrate. This alternative was a more accurate title, because his main tasks were to make sure the taxes were collected and to administer the law in his District.

There were 250 Districts in India in the late nineteenth century. The average size was 3,859 square miles and the average population 876,000. There were, however, wide variations. One District in Burma was nearly 20,000 square miles, about the size of Wales. Malabar District in Madras Province had over 2,650,000 people living in it.

The Princes

Large parts of India were not ruled directly by the British at all. These were the Princely states which remained the personal property of their Indian rulers. Some of these were small areas but a few were enormous (see map on page 9). In the south, Mysore and Travancore were large blocks of territory bordering Madras Province. The Prince who ruled Hyderabad, called the Nizam, owned an area larger than Great Britain. He was said to be the richest man in the world in his time, kept in the most luxurious style by the labours of his millions of subjects. He had a large army, splendid with elephants but useless for war, and an equally gorgeous state railway. Hyderabad City, with nearly half a million people living in it, was the fourth largest city in India.

But even the Nizam of Hyderabad had to accept the British as the real masters of India. The price of staying independent was to agree to have a British adviser at his side. Such advisers were called Residents and their job was to report back to their local Provincial Governors. Just by being there the Residents were a constant reminder to the Indian Princes of British power.

Men who became Residents were following one of the many careers open to members of the Indian Civil Service (ICS). Right through the first half of the nineteenth century all the District Officers, judges, Residents and so on were British. Most joined the ICS after spending a year or two at its College in Haileybury in England.

3
Indian Nationalism

The subcontinent of India has had a very long and varied history. Recorded civilisation goes back at least 6,000 years. Over that long period, kingdoms and empires have risen and fallen. There have been waves of invasions from the north. The most important of these took place around 1000 BC when Aryan invaders defeated local rulers and settled in much of north and central India. The people they defeated were the first settled Indians, the Dravidians, who they pushed south.

The most respected social group amongst the conquering Aryans were their priests, known as Brahmins. Next in rank came the warriors, the Kshatrias. Aryan society placed most people in groups, or castes, although some were outside the caste system altogether.

Much later the invasion of the Muslim Mughals in the early sixteenth century added another important piece to the complex pattern of Indian society. Caste had, in theory, no place in the social organisation of Muslim life. It is not difficult to see that with so many cultures and traditions, it was very hard for the various peoples of India to develop a sense of their common national traditions and culture.

Ram Mohan Roy

One of the first Indians to try to combine some of the ideas of the West with India's traditional way of life was the Bengali, Ram Mohan Roy (1772–1833). Born into a strict Brahmin Hindu family, he was interested in the religious and political ideas of Europeans. He supported English education and attacked some traditional Hindu ways. His family and friends criticised his attacks on what he called 'the peculiar practice of Hindoo idolatry' and on *suttee*, the ritual suicide of a widow on the funeral fire of her dead husband.

Hindu self-respect　At the same time, Roy was also critical of the behaviour of many Christian missionaries in Bengal and other parts of India. In 1823 he started a magazine *Being a Vindication of the Hindoo Religion Against the*

Attacks of Christian Missionaries which caused quite a stir in Calcutta. 'We have been subjected to such insults for about nine centuries,' he wrote. 'It seems almost natural that when one nation succeeds in conquering another, the former, though their religion may be quite ridiculous, laugh and despise the religion and manners of those that are fallen into their power.'

Roy served in the Indian Civil Service in Bengal (see page 10), rising as high as any Indian could at that time. Later he became a respected figure in Calcutta, influencing the next generation of Indian nationalists to believe that their culture and traditions were worthy of far more respect than that given them by the Europeans. In the last years of his life he went to England as an honoured visitor, dining with the Directors of the East India Company and acting as a sort of unofficial Indian ambassador. In 1833, he gave evidence to Parliament when it was considering whether to renew the Company's Charter (see page 7) and died later that year in Bristol.

Syed Ahmed Khan

Amongst that new generation was Syed Ahmed Khan, born into a powerful Delhi family in 1817. After a traditional Muslim education he worked for the East India Company, becoming a junior judge. The rebellion of 1857 in north India (see page 7) caused a great deal of mistrust between Muslims and the British, but Syed Ahmed saw that British rule was going to last a long time.

For the rest of his life he worked to get Muslims in India to put aside their dislike of the British and to become strong by taking advantage of the new education the British were offering in India. The handful of British could never rule in India on their own, of course. As government became more complicated there were more and more opportunities for Muslims and other Indians to find good jobs – but only if they had the educational qualifications wanted by the British.

Muslim self-respect

Syed Ahmed Khan talked, wrote and argued, stressing the importance of education and scientific knowledge. His greatest achievement was the founding of the Muhammadan Anglo-Oriental College in 1875, which was to become the Muslim University of Aligarh in 1921. Even though he was a fearless critic of the government he was so important a figure in the Muslim community that he was invited to serve on the Viceroy's Legislative Council from 1878 to 1882.

Syed Ahmed was attacked by some traditional Muslims, just as traditional Hindus had criticised Ram Mohan Roy. He wrote:

'I have been accused by people who do not understand of being disloyal to the culture of Islam, even to Islam itself.... Today there are no Muslim rulers to patronise [provide jobs for] those who are well versed in the old Arabic and Persian learning. The new rulers insist upon a knowledge of their language for all advancement in their services and in some of the independent professions like practising law as well. If the Muslims do not take the system of education introduced by the British, they will not only remain a backward community but will sink lower and lower until there is no hope of recovery left to them. Is this at all a pleasing prospect? Can we serve the cause of Islam this way?'

Syed Ahmed and his followers became a powerful influence on the Muslim community in the last decades of the nineteenth century and beyond. They, and their ideas, came to be called the Aligarh Movement. While they helped to build a new sense of identity in the Muslim community, it was not a part of defining an Indian nation. Syed Ahmed felt that the religion and history of the peoples of India were so different that they could never work together. At the back of his mind was the certain knowledge that Muslims would always be a minority in India as a whole.

The Indian National Congress

The political meeting for which the lawyers and doctors had come to Bombay on the train from Allahabad in 1885 (see page 2) was called by a retired British civil servant, Allan Hume. Earlier that year he had written a letter to former students of Calcutta University. In it he asked for fifty men 'with sufficient power of self-sacrifice, sufficient love

A group photograph of the delegates at the first Indian National Congress, 1885. Sessions were held annually and attracted representatives of the Indian middle classes. The number of delegates rose to 1200 by the fourth meeting held in 1888.

for and pride in their country . . . to devote the rest of their lives to the Cause.' The Cause was Indian nationalism. Hume was surprised and delighted by the number of replies he received. Seventy-two men attended that first meeting. They called themselves the Indian National Congress and Allan Hume was elected as their first General Secretary, a post he held for the next twenty-three years.

The major issue at this first meeting was entry to the Indian Civil Service. They wanted Indians to have a greater say in the way the country was run. The best way to achieve this, they felt, was to get far more Indians into the Civil Service. However, to enter you had to sit an examination in London, and the age limit for this had just been lowered to nineteen. Both of these things made it much harder for Indian men to compete successfully with British candidates. In Resolution IV the National Congress asked for examinations to be held in India as well as London and for a higher age limit. Within a few years both changes were made. It was a small but significant victory for Indian nationalism.

The first page of the Report of the First Indian National Congress held at Bombay on 28, 29 and 30 December, 1885.

SUMMARY

OF

RESOLUTIONS PASSED AT THE

FIRST INDIAN NATIONAL CONGRESS,

Composed of Representatives from Calcutta, Madras, Bombay, Poona, Allahabad, Lahore, Lucknow, Agra, Benares, Ahmedabad, Kurrachee, Surat, Veerumgaum, Ganjam, Masulipatam, Chingleput, Tanjore, Combaconum, Madras, Tinnevelly, Coimbatore, Cuddapah, Anantapoor, Bellary and Umballa,

HELD IN BOMBAY,

On the 28th, 29th and 30th December, 1885.

⤜◇⤛

RESOLUTION I.

Resolved.—That this Congress earnestly recommends that the promised inquiry into the working of Indian Administration, here and in England, should be entrusted to a Royal Commission, the people of India being adequately represented thereon, and evidence taken both in India and in England.

[Proposed by Mr. G. Subramania Iyer, (*Madras*) ; seconded by Mr. P. M. Mehta, (*Bombay*): and supported by Mr. Norendronath Sen, (*Calcutta*).]

RESOLUTION II.

Resolved.—That this Congress considers the abolition of the Council of the Secretary of State for India, as at present constituted, the necessary preliminary to all other reforms.

[Proposed by Mr. S. H. Chiplonkar, (*Poona*) ; seconded by Mr. P. Ananda Charlu, (*Madras*) ; and supported by Mr. J. Ghosal, (*Allahabad*).]

RESOLUTION III.

Resolved.—That this Congress considers the reform and expansion of the Supreme and existing Local Legislative Councils, by the admission of a considerable proportion of elected members (and the creation of similar Councils for the N.-W. Provinces and Oudh, and also for the Punjab) essential ; and holds that all Budgets should be referred to these Councils for consideration, their members being moreover empowered to interpellate the Executive in regard to all branches of the administration ; and that a Standing Committee of the House of Commons should be constituted to receive and consider any formal protests that may be recorded by majorities of such Councils against the exercise by the Executive of the power, which would be vested in it, of over-ruling the decisions of such majorities.

[Proposed by the Hon. K. T. Telang, C.I.E., (*Bombay*) ; seconded by the Hon. S. Subramania Iyer, (*Madras*) ; and supported by the Hon. Dadabhai Naoroji, (*Bombay*).]

RESOLUTION IV.

Resolved.—That in the opinion of this Congress the competitive examinations now held in England, for first appointments in various civil departments of the public service, should henceforth, in accordance with the views of the India Office Committee of 1860, ' be held simultaneously, one in England and one in India, both being as far as practicable identical in their nature, and those who compete in both countries being finally classified in one list according to merit,' and that the successful candidates in India should be sent to England for

Moderates and Extremists

By 1900 the Indian National Congress had increased its support throughout India. Its active members were mainly doctors, lawyers, teachers and other professional people. In the Bombay region, Indian businessmen were powerful supporters of the National Congress and so were a number of landowners in Bengal in the north-east. The leaders of Congress in these early years came to be called the Moderates because they wanted to use peaceful, moderate methods to get more say for Indians in the ruling of India. The leading figure amongst the Moderates was Gopal Krishna Gokhale.

Gokhale

Gokhale was born into a Brahmin family in Maharashtra, the area around Bombay in western India, in 1866. At the age of nineteen he decided to join the Deccan Education Society in Poona, a large town in the hills not far from Bombay. All members of this Society agreed, when they joined, to spend at least the next twenty years of their lives trying to achieve higher standards of education for Indians. Gokhale became a teacher of English and maths, working in a number of schools in Maharashtra. He was also by this time a very active member of the National Congress and in 1902 at the age of thirty-six he became the representative of the state of Bombay in the Imperial Legislative Council, the highest law-making body in the country. His slogan was 'No taxation without representation', meaning that it was unfair for Indians to pay taxes to the British for the ruling of India while they had almost no say in how the money was spent. The British were unwilling to give in to these demands and Gokhale exhausted himself in trying to organise campaigns until his death in 1915.

Gokhale and the Moderates were willing to work with the British in the hope of getting steady change but there were others in the National Congress who were less patient. They came to be called the Extremists and their leader was Bal Ganghadar Tilak.

Tilak

Tilak was also a Brahmin from Maharashtra and he too joined the Deccan Education Society. He resigned from the Society in 1890 because he did not think its polite, patient methods were working. He had been told many stories as a child of the greatness of the Marathas who had ruled a large area of western and central India before the British came. Tilak wanted to revive the nationalist feelings of the mass of ordinary Indians, pointing out to them how strong they once had been and how weak they had become. He wanted them to use their anger to take what he felt was theirs by right. Tilak spoke to villagers in Maharashtra in a direct, effective way. In the newspapers he himself started up he made his views widely known. He wrote a lot about the glories of the Hindu past and revived a religious festival in that western part of India in honour of Ganesh, the elephant-headed Hindu god.

In 1897 two British officials were murdered in Poona. Tilak was accused of stirring up public hatred of these officials in his newspapers and was sentenced to eighteen months in prison. This only seemed to make him more determined. 'Freedom is my birthright and I will have it,' he declared, and his words echoed around India.

In 1907 Tilak put his popularity to the test. He and some of his Extremist friends tried to get themselves elected to the top posts at the National Congress meeting of that year. They failed and the meeting ended in noisy confusion.

Tilak was arrested again by the British a short time later. He was accused of urging readers of his newspapers to use violence and assassination and found guilty. He was sentenced to six years in prison in Burma, far away from Maharashtra. He spent these years writing about the most popular religious poem of Hindus, the *Bhagavad Gita*.

Tilak died in 1920. By that time he had become rather less hostile towards the British but his fearless defiance is still well remembered in India today. He tried to make the cause of Indian nationalism something that ordinary men and women could understand and take part in. He is known today by the title Lokamanya – 'Honoured by the People'.

4
The Partition of Bengal

Bengal is a large area in the north-east of India wrapped around the top of the Bay of Bengal. The sacred river Ganges fans out in a wide swampy delta in this region to meet the sea. The soil is among the richest on earth.

In 1765 the Mughal Emperor granted the British East India Company the right to collect taxes in Bengal (see page 6). He had little choice because the Company and its troops had become the effective rulers of Bengal. In 1858 the powers of the Company were taken over by the British government directly. Calcutta, a city on the banks of the River Hooghly some eighty kilometres from the Bay of Bengal, became the capital of British India.

Partition

The British fixed the boundaries of their Province of Bengal to include not only Bengal itself but also two other large regions, Bihar and Orissa. In addition it contained the capital of the British government in India, Calcutta. In all, the Province of Bengal had a population of 78 million, twice as many as Britain at the time. One reason for the Partition plan was to divide up this large area and population so that it could be administered more effectively. There had been several different schemes for dividing the Province yet none of them took account of local opinion or political leaders.

Curzon's plan

In 1905 the Viceroy, Lord Curzon, decided to act. He created a new Province of East Bengal with its capital at Dacca. This area contained eastern Bengal and the tea-growing area of Assam and had a mainly Muslim population of some 30 million. The new, smaller Province of Bengal had a large majority of Hindus but the Bengalis there found themselves outnumbered by Biharis from Bihar and Oriyas from Orissa.

The British were not prepared for the storm of protest caused by this Partition plan. Many Bengalis, especially Hindus in the western parts, were sure that the British wanted to split Bengal mainly to divide and so weaken the voice of Bengal in Indian politics. There were demonstrations and marches. There was a widespread boycott of British goods and bales of cotton cloth from Lancashire were burned in the streets. The leader of this protest movement against Partition was Surendranath Banerjea.

Surendranath Banerjea

The story of Banerjea's political life is one of great determination in the face of major obstacles. A doctor's son, he was born in Bengal in 1848. He was one of the very first Indians to get into the ICS. His first posting was to Sylhet, a country area in the north-east of Bengal.

After a short time there, a clerk in his office wrote a report that was false. Banerjea signed his report and handed it in, the sort of mistake for which an English junior ICS officer would get no more than a friendly word of warning. Not in this case. Banerjea was sacked from the ICS and his appeal in London failed. It was a bitter experience and he wrote later that 'the personal wrong done me was an illustration of the impotency of our people.'

Banerjea determined to spend the rest of his life putting that right. He became a teacher, started a newspaper, then founded a college. He became the leading Congress politician in Bengal, with a national reputation. He was, in his long career in politics, put in jail more than once by the British but he always insisted on using peaceful and legal methods in the struggle for self-government. But even Banerjea was shocked by Curzon's Partition plan for Bengal. 'We have been insulted, humiliated and tricked,' he declared. He did realise, though, that in one way the Viceroy had helped the cause of Indian nationalism: 'Bad rulers are often a blessing in disguise. They help to stir a community into life, a result that years of agitation would perhaps have failed to achieve.'

Bande Mataram

'Surrender not' Banerjea, as he was often called by his supporters, was on the Moderate side of the Indian National Congress. In fact, the movement against the Partition of Bengal drew its power from the anger of many ordinary Indians. This mass politics had been the aim of the Extremists in the Indian National Congress. The Anti-Partition campaign in Bengal is a great landmark in the history of Indian nationalism, in which the methods of the Extremists proved highly effective.

To build up mass support for the nationalist movement, the members of Congress – mainly educated professionals – had to concentrate on the things they had in common with the mass of ordinary Indians. These were mainly language, history and religion. All three combined powerfully in the popular historical novels of the Bengali writer Bankim Chandra Chatterjee. His most famous novel *Anandamath* (The Abbey of Bliss) is about a rebellion in Bengal in the 1770s against the Mughals. In this book there is a poem, 'Bande Mataram' (Hail to the Mother). The 'Mother' is both the land of Bengal and the female aspect of the Hindu deity. This poem became the fighting song of the campaign against Partition in Bengal, and then the anthem of the whole Indian nationalist movement.

> Mother, I bow to thee!
> Rich with thy hurrying streams,
> Bright with thy orchard gleams,
> Cool with thy winds of delight,
> Dark fields waving, Mother of might,
> Mother free.

Hindus and Muslims

The campaign against Partition brought out into the open the tensions that had existed for a long time between Hindus and Muslims in Bengal.

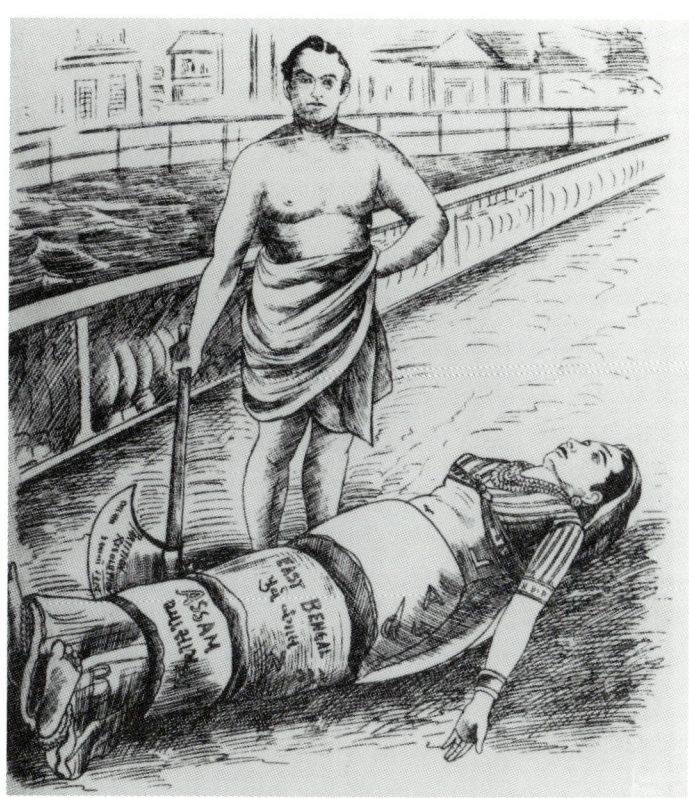

'Vandalism! or, the Partition of Bengal': a cartoon from Hindi Punch, *July 1905. Lord Curzon is the figure with the axe.*

The campaign itself was mostly a Hindu affair. It was young Bengalis from the Hindu community who joined physical fitness clubs, marched and sang patriotic songs. Rusty old family revolvers were taken from their hiding places and cleaned, ready for trouble. An attempt was made to blow up the train of the Lieutenant Governor of Bengal. A bomb meant for a judge killed two English women instead. The bombers became popular heroes for a while. Nirad Chaudhuri, a writer who was a boy in Bengal at the time, remembers how he and his brother built make-believe bombs out of coconut shells, charcoal and kerosene.

Many Muslims supported Partition. Most Muslim political leaders had not, in fact, joined the Indian National Congress and in December 1906 in Dacca they formed their own political party, the Muslim League. Nationalism in Bengal had always been affected by Hindu resentment of the Muslims who used to rule Bengal before the British came. The Partition campaign turned this resentment into open hostility. There was serious rioting in different parts of Bengal, as Muslim mobs took revenge for Hindu atrocities in a tragic spiral of violence that was to become all too familiar in the years ahead.

In 1907 Nirad Chaudhuri's class at school was split into two separate sections, one Hindu and one Muslim. No official explanation was given. Nobody seemed to be sorry.

Morley and Minto

In Britain the Liberal Party won a landslide victory in the general election of 1906. The Liberals had more sympathy for Indian nationalism than the previous Conservative government. They had been impressed by the strength of the campaign against Partition in Bengal. In particular they noted the tensions and violence between Muslim and Hindu communities during the campaign and the forming of the Muslim League.

The Liberals were determined to make changes in the way that the government reacted to Indian nationalism, in Bengal and elsewhere. The new Secretary of State for India, John Morley, wasted little time. He replaced the haughty Lord Curzon as Viceroy with Lord Minto, a cool but experienced colonial administrator.

The 'Reforms', 1909

Morley and Minto started talks with Gokhale and others about ways to involve Indians much more directly in the governing of India. The result of these talks was the Indian Councils Act of 1909, usually known as the Morley-Minto Reforms. The most important change was to the Imperial Legislative Council. This was the main law-making body in India. It was made much larger, with sixty rather than twenty-five members. Nearly half were to be directly elected Indian members. Legislative Councils in the provinces were also made much larger with many more Indians elected by the people of each province.

Indians could only vote in the new elections if they had a certain amount of property. Morley and Minto feared that Muslims in Bengal, who were usually poorer than Bengali Hindus, would not have many voters and that this would result in more division and violence. Because of these fears, a number of seats on the new, larger Councils were reserved for Indian Muslims. This was called 'communal representation'.

The British in India may have seemed very powerful but there were always very few of them trying to rule a vast and mixed population. Little in the way in which they had been trained helped them to understand or control the passions caused by Indians' religious beliefs.

After 1909 political life settled down in Bengal. Many leading nationalists, Hindus and Muslims, were elected to the new Councils. The campaign against Partition was won at last when the two parts of Bengal were put back together again in 1911. The Province lost some of its importance, however, because the capital of British India was moved from Calcutta to Delhi in the same year.

5

For King and Country

Late in the evening of 4th August, 1914, a royal proclamation came from Buckingham Palace. From eleven o'clock that evening Britain and her Empire were at war with Germany. The following morning in New Delhi, the capital of British India, the Viceroy Lord Hardinge passed on the dramatic news. 250 million of King George V's Indian subjects were now officially at war. Nobody asked them if they wanted to fight the Germans, a faraway people of whom they knew nothing. It was the same throughout the Empire, from Canada to Kenya, from Jamaica to Australia to New Zealand.

The Indian Army at war

In 1914 the Indian Army was about 150,000 strong. Its main task was to keep the peace on the North West Frontier, a job it did well. It was armed with out-of-date rifles and used mules for transport, an army for the defence of India. During the First World War this army swelled to ten times its peacetime size, fighting with great distinction in Europe and the Middle East.

When the Prince of Wales inspected the Bhopal Regiment in northern France at Christmas 1914 they were still in their usual lightweight khaki uniforms. Yet these men from the hot and dusty plains of central India earned a fine reputation in the murderous mud of trench warfare.

History does not do justice to the contribution of the Indian Army on the Western Front. Very few history books even mention it, but there is much to tell. The Garhwal Brigade was perhaps the most famous unit of the Indian Army there, winning three of the five Victoria Crosses awarded to Indian soldiers. The Brigade was made up of Garhwalis, tough mountainmen from the Himalayas, their neighbours the 2nd/3rd Gurkhas and the 2nd Leicesters from England. The Garhwalis arrived in France in October 1914 and were sent into action almost immediately. They dug trenches for twenty days without a break, often barelegged in icy water. Twenty years later Philip Mason,

Garhwalis on the La Bassee Road, France, during the war.

District Officer in Garhwal, was proudly shown feet without toes by Garhwali veterans of the trenches.

Divided loyalties

When war was declared in 1914 almost all official opinion in India was enthusiastic. More than 700 of India's Princes offered to help the war effort in some way, though not all went quite so far as the Maharaja of Rewa. He offered his troops, his land and his private jewels, and ended his telegram to London with 'What order has my King for me?' Messages of loyalty and support also came from the Congress Party in the United Provinces, from the Muslim League and the national voice of the Sikh community, the Khalsa Diwan.

As the war dragged on the political climate in India began to change. Many British officials and Indian political leaders saw the strains that the war was creating for Indian people. The submarine war in Europe meant that wheat needed for food in Punjab was being exported to Britain. Prices went up and there were shortages. More significantly, many Indians began to lose some illusions about Britain. The world war showed to many soldiers and others the sight of the great powers of Europe, who had for so long been Lords of Asia, tearing away at each other's throats. 'Village India', wrote one historian, 'saw Europe in its sordid wartime clothes and was not impressed with what it saw.' Indian troops returned to their villages with stories that British troops were not always victorious in battle. They could be beaten like anyone else. The military reputation of Britain in India was never the same again.

On the fringes of Indian politics a very few saw a chance to overthrow the British by armed struggle. An Indian Revolutionary Committee was formed in Berlin and the German government promised arms. Jatin Mukherji was chosen to lead the revolution. M. N. Roy was to collect the arms in Java but none arrived from Germany and the scheme collapsed.

Ghadrite rebellion

In Punjab in 1915 an attempted armed rebellion by the Ghadr party failed. The Ghadrites were almost all Sikhs who had formed their revolutionary party abroad, on the west coast of Canada and the USA, with the intention of driving the British out of India. They found little or no support from Sikhs in Punjab and they were easily rounded up by the police. Even so their actions show that not everyone was keen to support Britain's war effort. Rather, they saw wartime conditions as ideal for fighting for Independence for India. The Sikh historian Khushwant Singh has called the Ghadrite rebellion 'India's first armed rebellion'.

The Viceroy was so alarmed about the tense situation in Punjab, Bengal and elsewhere that an emergency law was announced in 1915, the Defence of India Act. This gave the government of India sweeping wartime powers of arrest and detention without trial.

The Home Rule League

The great majority of political groups in India rejected violence but most were certain that the political situation in India would never be the same as it had been before 1914. There was a growing feeling that Britain would have to reward India for her support and sacrifices during the war by giving Indians a much greater say in government when the war was over. The British did not see things in quite that way, so in 1916 an organisation was formed to press the British to give more political power to Indians. It was called the Home Rule League and its founders were Bal Ganghadar Tilak (see page 15) and Mrs Annie Besant.

Tilak and Besant

Gokhale, the Moderate leader in the Indian National Congress, had died the previous year (see page 15). Tilak was now without a rival as leading Congress politician. As for Mrs Besant, she had first come to the notice of the public as an organiser of the London Matchgirls' strike in 1888. After that she became a Theosophist, with a belief in a universal World Soul and in reincarnation, the rebirth of the souls of the dead in other bodies. She became the President of the Theosophical Society in 1907 and remained so until her death in 1933. She lived in

India from 1895, feeling that Theosophy and Hinduism had much in common. She helped to found the Hindu University at Benares (now Varanasi), the holy city on the River Ganges, and became well known in Indian politics.

The Lucknow Pact

Tilak used his dominant position in the Indian nationalist movement to lead the Extremists back into the Congress Party in December 1916. That same month he helped to bring Congress and the Muslim League together, working with Muhammad Ali Jinnah, the League leader. Congress and the League held a joint conference in Lucknow, southeast of Delhi. Here the two parties agreed to a plan for the future of India which together they would offer the British. This agreement is known as the Lucknow Pact. It was important not just because Congress and the League were working together but also because the plan involved carrying on with separate electorates for Muslims, an idea Congress had bitterly opposed in 1909. The Pact insisted that an early date be fixed for self-government for India.

Muhammad Ali Jinnah

Muhammad Ali Jinnah was born in Karachi in 1876. His father, a merchant, was just able to afford to send his son to England to train as a barrister. Jinnah had his first taste of politics as a young man in London, taking an interest in the Liberal Party.

When he returned to India in 1896 Jinnah moved down the coast to Bombay. After a few difficult years he became known there as the most able and successful young lawyer around. He now took up his interest in politics and joined the Indian National Congress. In 1909 he was elected to the Imperial Legislative Council by Bombay Muslims. His ability was soon noticed, especially by Gokhale who saw him as the ideal man to bring Muslims and Hindus together in the nationalist movement.

Jinnah joined the Muslim League in 1913 and three years later he was able to fulfil Gokhale's hopes by helping to bring the Muslim League and the Indian National Congress together in the Lucknow Pact. In 1917 Edwin Montagu, the Secretary of State for India, went to the subcontinent to talk to political leaders there. He describes a meeting he and the Viceroy, Lord Chelmsford, had with the Muslim lawyer:

'They were followed by Jinnah, young, perfectly mannered, impressive looking, armed to the teeth with arguments.... I was rather tired but Chelmsford tried to argue with him, and was tied in knots. Jinnah is a very clever man, and it is, of course, an outrage that such a man should have no chance of running the affairs of his own country.'

Edwin S. Montagu, *An Indian Diary*, 1931.

6

'A derelict nation'

Peace came in 1918. Most soldiers returned to their peacetime lives in villages and towns. During the war higher taxes, shortages of essentials like kerosene and higher prices had made life difficult for ordinary Indians. Food prices had nearly doubled. After the war prices kept on rising. By 1920, they were on average two and half times higher than they had been in 1910.

Some had done well, especially industrialists. One mill owner in Ahmedabad trebled his profits in 1917–18. But for those on low fixed incomes, including government clerks, times were hard. There were many reports of small-scale riots and disturbances all over India, but they were local affairs which did not seriously challenge British rule.

It was a different matter when questions were asked about how India as a whole was to be governed. Things could not return to the way they had been in 1914. India's huge contribution to the war effort had to count for something. This was a war in defence of freedom. What about freedom for India? Jawaharlal Nehru, looking back on this period, wrote:

'World War I ended at last and the peace, instead of bringing us relief and progress, brought us repressive legislation and Martial Law in the Punjab. A bitter sense of humiliation and a passionate anger filled our people.... We had become a derelict nation.'

J. Nehru, *The Discovery of India*, 1945.

Montagu and Chelmsford

Edwin Montagu became Secretary of State for India in May 1917. The Home Rule League had forced the government to realise that changes had to come in the way India was governed. A few months later Montagu announced that the government wanted 'the increasing association of Indians in every branch of administration and the gradual development of self-governing institutions'. This was the first time in 150 years of British rule that British policy for the future of India had ever been stated. In plain language it meant slow and steady progress towards a time when India would be governed by Indians. Nationalists in India liked the sound of this but many were worried at the lack of a timetable for these changes. Britain would set the pace.

Dyarchy

The first changes were, in fact, not long coming. The powers and staff of the Viceroy stayed the same but at the next level down, in the various provinces, the tasks of government were split into two groups. Education, Public Health and Public Works were to be put in the charge of elected Indian ministers, although the Governor of the

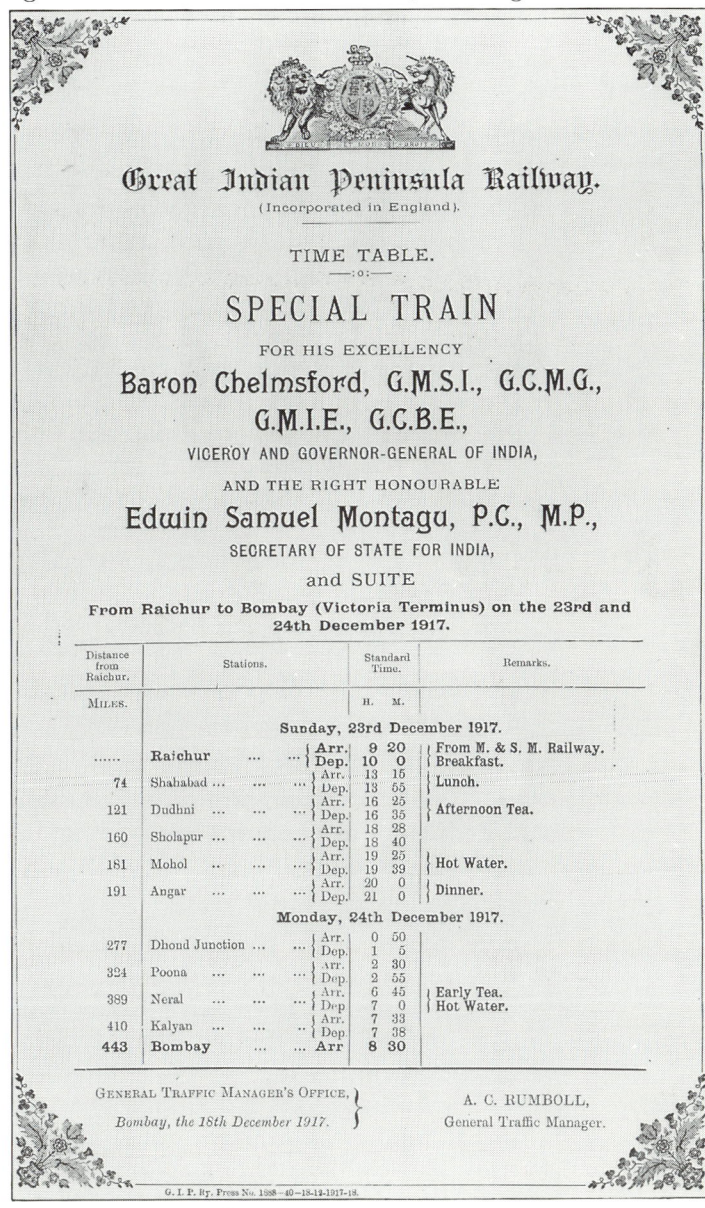

Great Indian Peninsula Railway.
(Incorporated in England).

TIME TABLE.
—:o:—

SPECIAL TRAIN

FOR HIS EXCELLENCY

Baron Chelmsford, G.M.S.I., G.C.M.G.,
G.M.I.E., G.C.B.E.,

VICEROY AND GOVERNOR-GENERAL OF INDIA,

AND THE RIGHT HONOURABLE

Edwin Samuel Montagu, P.C., M.P.,

SECRETARY OF STATE FOR INDIA,

and SUITE

From Raichur to Bombay (Victoria Terminus) on the 23rd and 24th December 1917.

Distance from Raichur.	Stations.		Standard Time.		Remarks.
MILES.			H.	M.	
					Sunday, 23rd December 1917.
......	Raichur	Arr.	9	20	From M. & S. M. Railway.
		Dep.	10	0	Breakfast.
74	Shahabad	Arr.	13	15	Lunch.
		Dep.	13	55	
121	Dudhni	Arr.	16	25	Afternoon Tea.
		Dep.	16	35	
160	Sholapur	Arr.	18	28	
		Dep.	18	40	
181	Mohol	Arr.	19	25	Hot Water.
		Dep.	19	39	
191	Angar	Arr.	20	0	Dinner.
		Dep.	21	0	
					Monday, 24th December 1917.
277	Dhond Junction	Arr.	0	50	
		Dep.	1	5	
324	Poona	Arr.	2	30	
		Dep.	2	55	
389	Neral	Arr.	6	45	Early Tea.
		Dep.	7	0	Hot Water.
410	Kalyan	Arr.	7	33	
		Dep.	7	38	
443	Bombay	Arr	8	30	

GENERAL TRAFFIC MANAGER'S OFFICE,
Bombay, the 18th December 1917.

A. C. RUMBOLL,
General Traffic Manager.

G. I. Ry. Press No. 1938—40–18-12-1917-18.

Montagu was invited to India by Chelmsford and after a preliminary conference in Delhi they toured the country, visiting Calcutta, Madras and Bombay. This timetable shows part of the route to Bombay. Montagu returned to England at the end of April 1918 after further talks.

province remained in overall charge. The police, the courts and the taxation of land remained the direct responsibility of the Governor. This shared system of government was known as 'dyarchy', rule by two groups. Real power stayed firmly in British hands but it was still a big step forward and generally welcomed in India. Most ICS officers accepted that the changes were needed.

These changes are often known as the Montagu-Chelmsford Reforms. Secretary of State Montagu and the Viceroy, Lord Chelmsford, may have announced the changes but the creators of change, of the moral and political pressures that brought them about, were the hundreds of thousands of Indian soldiers who had fought and died for the British Empire. The changes became law in the Government of India Act of 1919.

The Rowlatt Acts

The activities of the small revolutionary groups in India during the war had been easily dealt with. After the war was over, many officials wanted to keep in place the war-time powers of arrest and detention made possible by The Defence of India Act (see page 24), to give them power to deal with political protest. They realised that passing a law to keep these powers in their hands would be much harder when more Indians were involved in making important decisions in India under the Montagu-Chelmsford Reforms.

In 1917 a committee was set up in India under a Scottish judge, A. T. S. Rowlatt. Its task was 'to investigate revolutionary conspiracies'. Rowlatt's report came a year later. It identified Bengal, Bombay and Punjab as dangerous centres of conspiracy and recommended emergency powers in these areas to deal with this.

Edwin Montagu, the Secretary of State in London, distrusted the evidence Rowlatt gave for his recommendation. He told Lord Chelmsford, the Viceroy, that Rowlatt's suggestions were 'most repugnant'. He wanted to deal with any threats of revolution, of course, but he believed the due process of law must be used:

> 'I loathe the suggestion at first sight of preserving the Defence of India Act in peace time to such an extent as Rowlatt and his friends think necessary.'

Despite Montagu's objections, the leading officials in India were determined to get these laws passed before the Montagu-Chelmsford Reforms made it impossible to do so. They used their built-in majority on the Imperial Legislative Council (see page 8). The Rowlatt laws were passed even though every Indian member of this Council voted against them.

The Indian National Congress was, of course, also completely opposed to these new laws but disagreed about the best tactics to use against them. Most were so angry that they demanded a campaign of civil disobedience – public protest that would break the law and lead to mass arrests. Others spoke against this plan, fearing mass violence. The person who emerged to lead the civil disobedience campaign was a lawyer from Gujarat, Mohandas Gandhi.

Massacre at Amritsar

The campaign against the Rowlatt Acts began with a 24-hour general strike or *hartal*. April 6th, 1919 was the chosen day. All shops and businesses would close. Gandhi wanted dignified protest, with prayer, fasting and bathing, but there were many violent disturbances in various parts of India. Government buildings were burned and officials were attacked. Shops and homes were looted. Trains were stopped and telephone wires were cut. Many people died in riots. Gandhi was horrified and called for an end to the *hartal* but the violence continued.

Some of the worst rioting had been in the city of Amritsar in Punjab, the holy city of the Sikh religion. On 10th April an English woman schoolteacher was attacked by a crowd. She was not killed but the authorities in Punjab were determined to get tough. The new army commander in the area, Brigadier-General Reginald Dyer, ordered a total ban on public meetings. But on 13th April some 5,000 people met at Jallianwalla Bagh, an open space almost entirely surrounded by buildings.

General Dyer blocked the entrance to this space with troops. Without trying to get the crowd to disperse he ordered his men to open fire. For ten minutes the firing continued. When it stopped, nearly 500 lay dead. 1,200 were wounded. All were unarmed men, women and children.

The next day, with brutal insensitivity, General Dyer ordered that all Indians passing the place where the English teacher had been attacked must crawl on their hands and knees. Refusal meant a public beating. Dyer's brutality matched the strongest statements of Indian nationalists about the depths to which some British could descend. The Amritsar Massacre sent waves of shock and anger around India, and remains a landmark in the struggle for independence.

Most British were horrified too and the government acted quickly. Dyer was relieved of his command and faced a court martial. An enquiry made it clear that he had acted on his own initiative, but the damage had been done. The army decided that Dyer had to retire on half pay. This was bitterly resented in India, where it was thought that retirement from military service was hardly adequate punishment. The bitterness was increased by the support given to Dyer's actions by some British politicians, especially in the House of Lords.

The Imperial tango

In practice the Montagu-Chelmsford reforms were a big step forward in India. The new system of dyarchy worked quite well in the Pro-

Amritsar: the narrow entrance leading to Jallianwalla Bagh where Dyer stationed his troops.

vincial Governments. It would have worked much better but for the angry protests against the Rowlatt Acts which were written into the Government of India Act. This was poor timing by the British as it raised the political temperature at just the wrong time. The Indian National Congress voted against accepting the Montagu-Chelmsford changes even if it was by a narrow majority. They decided not to join the new legislative assemblies. It was the old Imperial Tango, two steps forward and one step back.

7

Mahatma Gandhi

Mohandas Karamchand Gandhi was born on 2nd October, 1869 in Porbandar, a small town on the coast of Gujarat. His family belonged to a trading caste but both his father and his grandfather had been Chief Minister to the rulers of a number of the small independent states in that part of north-west India.

Mohandas had three sisters and two brothers, all older than himself. He wrote later that his father was 'truthful, brave and generous but short-tempered'. He had little education but a great deal of practical experience, dealing with complicated law cases and organising hundreds of men. Mohandas remembered his mother for her strong common sense and her intelligence, but above all for what he called her 'saintliness'. 'She was deeply religious,' he wrote. 'She would take the hardest vows and keep them without flinching. Illness was no excuse for relaxing them.'

School and marriage

At his primary school Mohandas worked hard but was painfully shy and never talked to anyone if he could avoid it. When he was twelve he went on to high school.

His only close friend at school was much bigger, stronger and more confident than Mohandas. He did not have a good reputation. His mother warned him against this friendship but Mohandas said he hoped to improve this boy's character. Mohandas was afraid of many things. He could not sleep without a light for fear of snakes, ghosts and robbers. His friend had the answer. Meat. Meat-eating would make Mohandas much bigger and stronger and afraid of nothing, just like him. Look at the English, he said. Great strapping fellows, meat-eaters to a man. That's why they rule in India!

Mohandas, like many people in Gujarat, had been brought up a strict vegetarian but his friend persuaded him. For a while he did eat meat, secretly, deceiving his parents. After a while he stopped and was bitterly ashamed of his meat-eating and deceit for the rest of his life. Other painful memories of this time were of stealing small sums of money from house servants to buy cigarettes and even stealing a piece of gold from a bracelet belonging to his brother. When he handed his father a written confession asking to be punished for his crime his ill father sat up in his sick bed, read the note in silence and then tore it up gently, the paper wet from his father's tears. 'If I were a painter I could draw a picture of the whole scene today' he wrote forty years later.

After one year at high school, Mohandas was married. In India at that time marriage at an early age was quite common. Mohandas was just thirteen, the same age as Kasturba, the wife chosen for him by the elders of his family. A wedding for Mohandas suited the family at this time because both his elder brother and a cousin were to be married. Food, clothes and entertainment all cost a great deal of money, so it made sense to the family to have three weddings in one.

Later in his life Mohandas came to think that child marriages were very wrong but at the time he accepted without question the wishes of the family elders. Mohandas and Kasturba took the traditional seven steps together and made the traditional promises to each other. Their long married lives had begun.

Kasturba could neither read nor write. Mohandas was keen to help her but she was not very interested. There were strict rules in that part in India about how much time even married couples could spend together. 'I dared not meet her in the presence of the elders, much less talk to her,' he wrote later. Lessons were impossible. Mohandas had firm ideas about how a wife should behave. He tried to stop her seeing her friends but she did so anyway and they quarrelled, not speaking to each other for days. They were just sixteen when their first child died after living for only a few days. Two years later Mohandas was to go away to England, leaving Kasturba to look after their three-month-old son.

A passage to England

Mohandas left school and went on to a local college when he was eighteen. After just one term there he gave up and returned to his home. He had found the work too difficult and he was making no progress. His father had died two years before so the family turned to an old friend for advice on what Mohandas should do now. The Gandhis of Porbandar had a high reputation to keep up, advised the family friend, and Mohandas was the one to do it. If he was to be a Chief Minister like his father, his uncle and his grandfather before him, he must have qualifications. Times were changing. Mohandas should go to England and qualify as a barrister in London. Then he could return to India and expect to take his pick of important and well-paid jobs.

Mohandas was very keen to go but there were problems. The plan would cost the family a lot of money. Mohandas suggested selling his wife's jewelry. His elder brother thought they would manage to find the money somehow. An even bigger problem was that some in his family and caste did not think it right for him to go to England. His mother did not want her son to be away from home for so long. Anyway, she had heard that in England young men ate meat, drank alcohol, smoked cigars and kept bad company. Mohandas took a solemn vow not to touch wine, women or meat in England. His mother reluctantly agreed he could go.

Mohandas left home to take ship for England from Bombay. He had to wait there for several months and in that time his caste association tried to prevent him from going to England. Nobody from his caste had been before. How could he dare? To cross the sea was against his religion, they said. He would have to eat and drink with Europeans and that would be quite wrong. The whole idea was just not proper and decent!

A general meeting of the caste was called. Mohandas was ordered to attend. He defended his plan to go to England, saying it was not against his religion. He mentioned the vows he had taken for his mother but they would not listen. Mohandas said he would go anyway, that it was none of their business. In their anger the caste association then said he was expelled from the caste, an outcaste. Any other member of the caste who helped him or even saw him off at the docks would be fined. Mohandas did not give in to this pressure. He was more determined than ever to carry out his plan. At long last, in September 1887, he sailed for England.

The barrister

Mohandas Gandhi came ashore at Southampton a few weeks later. He lived with a family for a time but then moved into a room of his own. He was determined to keep the vow he had made to his mother and not eat meat. He had been surprised and delighted to find in London a number of vegetarian restaurants. He joined the Vegetarian Society and went to all their meetings but was too shy to speak.

It was also in London that he first read the *Bhagavad Gita*, the most popular religious poem of Hindus. Two English friends were reading the *Gita* in an English translation and they asked Mohandas to read it with them in its original language, Sanskrit. He knew enough to be thrilled by the *Gita*.

Gandhi went to England to qualify as a barrister at law. The course lasted for three years. Many law students skipped through their course but he read every word of the fat textbooks on the Common Law of England. It took him nine months of hard labour but he passed his final exams and in the middle of June 1891 qualified as a barrister. He left England the next day on the steamship *Assam* bound for Bombay.

In South Africa

Gandhi did not do well as a barrister in Bombay. He decided to try his luck back in Rajkot near his home but things were not much better there. The large trading company of Dada Abdulla, based in nearby Porbandar, had important links with South Africa and a big branch there. They had become involved in a major legal action in the South African courts. They offered Gandhi £105 and a first class return passage to South Africa if he would help in the presentation of their case there. Gandhi eagerly accepted this chance to get himself out of a rut and in April 1893 he sailed from Bombay to try his luck in South Africa.

Gandhi (centre) seated outside his office in South Africa around 1900. Notice his western clothes. What is there in the photograph to suggest that he was relatively successful as an attorney in South Africa?

It suited white South Africans to think of Indians in four groups. Muslim merchants were known as 'Arabs'. They were expected to wear turbans and could wear them in court. Then there were clerks of the Parsi religion, known as 'Persians'. Next came a fairly small number of Hindu clerks. These three groups had little contact with the fourth and much the largest group. These were either 'indentured' labourers, who had signed an agreement or 'indenture' to come to South Africa from India to work as contract labour in the sugar cane and tea plantations of Natal for five years, or freed labourers who had stayed on. They called themselves *girmitiyas* from *girmit*, a version of the word 'agreement'.

The agreement gave this group very few rights in South Africa. The system was the next thing to slavery and existed for the same reason, to provide cheap labour for plantations. South African whites used to call these workers 'coolies' which comes from an Indian word for an unskilled labourer. Because most Indians in South Africa belonged to this group, they came to use the term 'coolie' for all Indians. So Abdulla Sheth, who ran the Dada Abdulla family business, was a 'coolie merchant' and Gandhi became 'The Coolie Barrister'.

Gandhi stayed in Pretoria for a year. When the law case involving Dada Abdulla was settled, he set out for Durban, expecting to go back to India. Abdulla Sheth persuaded him to stay on in Durban to fight against a new law proposed in Natal in 1894. This law took away the franchise, or right to vote, from Indians living in Natal. Gandhi was just the man to organise the campaign against this new law. He had just been accepted as a full member of the Supreme Court of Natal, despite attempts to prevent this.

Two very busy years followed. Gandhi organised petitions and set up the Natal Indian Congress as a permanent organisation to fight for the rights of Indians in Natal. He was now getting plenty of cases and was well established in the community. It was time to return to India to fetch his wife, Kasturba and their children. Gandhi also wanted to bring conditions in South Africa to the attention of Indian nationalists. In the middle of 1896 he took a ship from Durban, landing in Calcutta a few weeks later.

The Green Pamphlet

Gandhi crossed India by train from Calcutta to Bombay and went on to Rajkot. He spent a few weeks writing a pamphlet which set out the facts about the conditions of Indians in South Africa. It became known as the Green Pamphlet from the colour of its cover. Gandhi had 10,000 copies printed and sent to every newspaper in India and to every important political leader.

Gandhi used the pamphlet as a way of meeting many of the leading nationalists. In Bombay he met the famous barrister Sir Pherozeshah Mehta, known to his many admirers as 'The Lion of Bombay'. Mehta was very helpful, arranging a public meeting, but Gandhi was so nervous when his time came to speak that few could hear his weak voice. After a while he gave up and handed his speech to another who read it for him.

Gandhi went to Poona, in the Hindu heartland of Maharashtra, to meet Tilak and Gokhale, the two famous nationalist leaders (see page 15). Gandhi had not met either of them before. Tilak he found rather a daunting character. Gokhale, by contrast, welcomed him as if they had been friends for years. 'Sir Pherozeshah had seemed to me like the Himalaya, Tilak like the ocean,' he wrote later, 'but Gokhale was as the Ganges. One could have a refreshing bath in the holy river.'

In Madras, in the south, Gandhi had a very warm welcome. His work on behalf of indentured labourers in Natal, many of whom came from Madras Province, was well known there. 10,000 of a new edition of the Green Pamphlet were printed. In Calcutta, however, it was a different story. He received a cold reception from politicians and newspaper editors alike. Surendranath Banerjea, the leading nationalist in Bengal, told him, 'I am afraid people will not take interest in your work. As you know, our difficulties here are by no means few.'

INDIANS IN NATAL.

SIMLA, SEPT. 12.

A pamphlet published by a native gentleman lately returned from South Africa has attracted some attention, as it describes the manner in which Indians are treated in Natal. The picture drawn is a sensational one, as it is alleged that the railway and tramcar officials treat the Indians like beasts, the hotel proprietors refuse to receive them, and the vagrant laws are very oppressive. The system of passes is strongly protested against as an interference with the personal liberty of the subject, while it is asserted that Indians are constantly robbed and assaulted and can obtain no redress from the magistracy.

The *Times of India* thinks that the grievances call urgently for redress, and advocates an official inquiry.

The *Pioneer* doubts if any good result would follow such an inquiry, as the colonists are stubborn folk and are not inclined to pay much respect to the Colonial Office at any time. It thus sums up the position :—

" A *de jure* relaxation of disabilities would benefit the natives of India nothing as long as the whole sentiment of the colonists is against them.

An article in The Times, *14 September 1896, commenting on the publication of the Green Pamphlet. What does the article reveal about the feelings of certain groups in India towards colonists and colonialism in general.*

Gandhi returned to Durban by sea from Bombay in December 1896. This time Kasturba, his two children and his nephew went with him. In his few months in India, he had become known to the country's leading nationalists and gained respect for his campaigns against the poor conditions of Indians in South Africa. He had made his mark.

Satyagraha

In 1907 the government in the South African Transvaal passed a new law, the Asiatic Registration Act. This meant that all Indians in the Transvaal had to be fingerprinted, registered and carry passes at all times. Gandhi led a campaign against this racist law. He went to London in 1909 to protest to the British government, but without success. Back in South Africa in 1913 a judge declared that only Christian marriages were considered to be legal in South Africa. Many Indian women, including Kasturba Gandhi, were outraged and joined the campaign. Gandhi and his followers marched, demonstrated and deliberately broke laws against moving around within South Africa because they thought them unjust. There were arrests, trials and imprisonments but the campaign attracted worldwide attention. At last, in June 1914, General Smuts, the Prime Minister of South Africa, asked to talk to Gandhi. A compromise agreement was reached between them. Many internal migration laws remained but non-Christian marriages were to be recognised as legal again.

Organised but non-violent resistance to unjust laws was not new but Gandhi had no equal in the skilful use of these tactics. In 1906 he and his followers had moved to Phoenix Farm near Durban. Here they printed the weekly newspaper *Indian Opinion* which Gandhi had started a few years earlier. He ran a competition in the newspaper to invent a word for the vigorous but non-violent campaigns he knew would be needed to fight unfair laws.

The winning entry came from Maganlal Gandhi, a young relative and co-worker of Gandhi's. It was *satyagraha*, from the word *sat*, meaning truth, and *agraha*, meaning firmness. Led by Gandhi, *satyagraha* campaigns proved to be highly effective in South Africa and later in India.

In 1914, two weeks after the success of the *satyagraha* campaign against the government, Gandhi left South Africa for good with his family. He had mixed feelings, excitement at the prospect of campaigning in India with Gokhale but regret at leaving South Africa 'where I had passed twenty years of my life sharing to the full in the sweets and bitters of human experience, and where I had realised my vocation in life.'

8
'Hind Swaraj'

'The Gujarati equivalent for civilisation means "good conduct"...
India has nothing to learn from anybody else and this is as it should
be.' Gandhi wrote this in a book in 1909 during a sea voyage from
London to South Africa. He gave it the title *Hind Swaraj*. In the Hindi
language *Hind* is a word for India. *Swaraj* is a word meaning 'self-rule'.
So *Hind Swaraj* means self-rule for India. It became a ringing political
slogan for Indian nationalists. Gandhi was telling them that they could
rely on their own traditions and need pay no attention to Western ideas
about what sorts of societies people should live in and which forms of
government were best.

For Gandhi the phrase had an important second meaning. He wrote:
'Real home-rule is self-rule or self-control.' Only when individuals were
able to control their own anger and other passions could they channel
these into effective campaigns. This was the basis of *satyagraha* (see
page 37).

Champaran and Kheda

Gandhi and his family had arrived in London in August 1914, just
after the declaration of war with Germany. Patriotism was infectious
and Gandhi, as a loyal subject of the King Emperor, did not take
advantage of war-time conditions for his political campaigns. He was
given a big welcome when he arrived in Bombay the following January
and had many offers of support, from his hero Gokhale and from a
number of wealthy Gujarati cotton mill owners.

Gokhale, who died early in 1915, had advised Gandhi to get to know
India better. Gandhi found that he was especially welcome in Madras
Province, from where so many of South Africa's indentured workers
came. In 1917, a poor farmer from Champaran, a remote district in the
north of Bihar, persuaded him to go there to help. The tenant farmers
were being mistreated by their mainly British landlords. Gandhi was
able to intervene and some changes were made. At the end of 1917 he
was called back to Gujarat to try and settle an industrial dispute

between owners and workers in Ahmedabad. Gandhi talked to both owners and workers and suggested some compromises. When these failed the following year the workers came out in a well-organised strike. Gandhi put great pressure on the owners by announcing that he would fast, to the death if necessary, until they agreed to take the dispute to arbitration. After three days they gave in. Gandhi had found a weapon of great power.

Soon after his fast, in March 1918, Gandhi organised the first effective full-scale *satyagraha* campaign. Bad weather the previous year meant that farmers in the Kheda District of Gujarat could not pay the usual taxes. The government insisted that they should pay. In reply Gandhi organised a *satyagraha* movement in which thousands took part. That was a great success but when Gandhi tried to recruit soldiers in the same area he had no success at all. He became dispirited, then ill. The campaign in Gujarat turned out to be only a rehearsal for the widespread protest which broke out in March 1919, when the government in India issued the Rowlatt Acts as law (see page 28). To Gandhi this was the sort of situation where *satyagraha* was the best tactic. With the *hartal* (or strike) he organised on 6th April along *satyagraha* lines, Gandhi's position amongst Indian nationalists was strengthened.

The ashram at Sabarmati

When Gandhi returned from South Africa in 1915, many from Phoenix Farm came with him. A merchant from Ahmedabad gave them land, an empty plot without trees or buildings. Here the group created an ashram. An ashram is a community, usually of a teacher, or guru, and his followers. The ashram on the Sabarmati River near Ahmedabad became home for Gandhi, his friends and followers, from 1917. It was a quiet spot, right on the river bank. It was near to Sabarmati Central Jail, too, and Gandhi thought this very proper for a community of *satyagrahi* very likely to end up in jail from time to time.

The forty founders of the ashram had to clear the ground. Gandhi had always feared snakes but he would allow none to be killed. Simple buildings were put up, including a school for weaving. Everyone ate together, shared their possessions and followed Gandhi's strict rules of diet and cleanliness.

Gandhi believed in being self-sufficient in as many things as possible. He wanted this not only for himself and his ashram but for India as a whole. He also wanted to rebuild India's traditional ways of earning a living. In Gujarat that had meant spinning and weaving. Soon the ashram was beginning to produce its own cotton cloth, a type called *Khadi*.

The ashram at Sabarmati was more than a home for Gandhi. After a campaign he would return to the ashram often bruised, often exhausted, to regain his strength amongst family and friends. One such time was after the campaign against the Rowlatt Acts had turned to violence on both sides. Gandhi had been horrified. He called it later 'a Himalayan

A general view of the Sabarmati valley. The picture gives an idea of the simplicity and peacefulness of the ashram there which Gandhi found so soothing.

blunder'. In the weeks after the violence he was restored by the daily routine there – the simple, shared life.

'Reforms' rejected   In 1920 Gandhi persuaded the Indian National Congress to reject the changes suggested by the government in the Montagu-Chelmsford Reforms (see page 26). Many in Congress wanted to join the new Legislative Assemblies and take advantage of more ICS places for Indians, but Gandhi persuaded a narrow majority to say no. He also got Congress to agree to boycott the courts, British schools and colleges and British goods, especially cloth – as well as the English language. This represented a major change in Congress thinking. The organisation was no longer the mouthpiece of lawyers and other professional people – mostly English educated. The final step to becoming a mass movement came later when Gandhi's supporters forced the Congress to accept a new constitution. The membership subscription was cut to an amount that almost all could afford. Congress was becoming a mass party.

The new constitution committed Congress to campaigns of non-cooperation. The first got under way in 1921. Gandhi travelled the country, by rail and on foot. In cities, towns and remote villages he drew large and enthusiastic crowds, a distinctive figure with his shaven head and spectacles, wearing only a white homespun loincloth. At first the government did not take the campaign seriously, becoming alarmed only when anti-British demonstrations greeted the Prince of Wales on his visit to India in 1921. The government ordered meetings to be broken up and Congress offices searched. By early 1922 around 30,000 Congress workers were in jail. Then in February in Chauri Chaura, a small village in the United Provinces, the villagers set fire to the local police station and twenty-one Indian policemen were burned to death. Gandhi stopped the civil disobedience campaign immediately.

Even so, in March the British arrested him at Sabarmati and tried him on a charge of writing newspaper articles encouraging people to rebel. He was found guilty and sentenced to six years in jail, but only served twenty-two months before being released to have an operation for appendicitis. Very weak and exhausted, he returned to the ashram at Sabarmati.

The march to the sea

At his trial in 1922 Gandhi declared: 'In my humble opinion, non-cooperation with evil is as much a duty as cooperation with good.' For almost everyone else involved the issues were not nearly so clear-cut as this. The British would not accept that their government was evil, although the more sensitive officials knew that changes had to come. They found it difficult to deal with the *satyagraha* campaigns and their methods were often clumsy and unnecessarily violent.

Gandhi had Indian critics, too. Some leading members of the National Congress wanted to work for change by joining the new Legislative Councils and many did. Others supported the idea of non-cooperation but could not agree that students should not attend British-run schools or colleges, or that it made sense to burn heaps of Lancashire cotton cloth in the streets. Rabindranath Tagore, the world famous poet and writer from Bengal, felt this very strongly. With Gandhi in prison, the non-cooperation movement came to a halt under these pressures.

The Simon Commission

Early in 1928 the British government sent a Commission of Enquiry to India led by Sir John Simon. The Commissioners' task was to look into the relationship between Britain and India and to recommend any changes they thought were needed. The Simon Commission said they wanted to hear from all groups in India but Gandhi and other Congress leaders refused to talk to them. They pointed out that there were no Indian members of the Simon Commission, and anyway, they said, the British would never give up real power in India. There were large protest meetings and demonstrations against the Simon Commission in 1928. The police made free use of their *lathis* – long and heavy iron-bound sticks – to break up crowds. In one police *lathi* charge, Lala Lajpat Rai, the nationalist leader in Punjab, was fatally injured. In retaliation the Assistant Commissioner of Police in Lahore, capital of Punjab, was assassinated and the Legislative Assembly in Delhi was bombed. Once again peaceful protest had ended in violence and death. Gandhi was appalled.

Many Congress leaders wanted independence for India, *Hind Swaraj*, right away without more discussions. Gandhi still wanted to keep a strong link with Britain and pressed for Dominion status, a form of self-government. He threatened that if Britain failed to give India Dominion status within a year, he would personally lead a national civil disobedience campaign for complete independence. In Britain the new Labour government led by Ramsay MacDonald suggested, in 1929, a Round Table Conference on India to take place in London the following year. Nationalists were split about how to react. Go to London or stay away? Dominion status or full independence? And what to do about the rulers of India's many Princely states? At last Congress cut through this knot. They decided to go for full independence. On 1st January 1930, Congress announced their decision. They called on all their members to back a national campaign for full independence, to be led by Gandhi. They wanted an issue to draw in the widest support and they found it in salt.

Salt taxes

Since ancient times, taxing salt had been the most widely-used way for governments to collect money from ordinary people. Salt was still taxed in British India and the money raised by this tax was an important part of government revenue. A third of all the salt used in India was produced by government workers. Another third was in the hands of private producers and a third was imported mainly from Aden and Britain. A number of other countries taxed salt in this way. In China the salt tax was the main source of government revenue. It was cheap and easy to collect and it had been there for as long as anyone could remember.

Gandhi did not accept this government argument. The salt tax was, he felt, unjust. Sea salt was a gift of nature and Gandhi realised that he could make the government look mean and unjust to the outside world by deliberately and publicly breaking the law about making salt. The government would have to arrest large numbers. Here was an ideal issue for a *satyagraha* campaign. He arranged the publicity with his usual skill. It was to be a symbolic gesture. He announced that he personally would lead a march from his ashram to the sea, 200 miles to the south of Sabarmati at a place called Dandi. There they would break the Salt Acts by making salt from the sea on the beach without paying the tax.

Gandhi set out with his followers on March 12th. As they marched south through the villages and towns of southern Gujarat, huge crowds turned out, some joining the marching column. Some journalists who had been invited along helped to spread the news of the march. The small wiry figure of Mahatma Gandhi in his homespun *dhoti*, striding at the head of his followers, captured the attention of India and the world. (Mahatma is a title of honour used by Hindus, given to those who are known for their wisdom or moral and spiritual qualities.)

They reached Dandi on April 5th. They camped on the beach and for the next month they made and sold small quantities of salt. They waited to see how the government would react. At first nothing happened at all, but all over India, as news of the Salt March spread, other marches began to take place, large and small. On the coasts, thousands made and sold salt until the campaign against the Salt Acts had become much more widespread than any of Gandhi's earlier *satyagraha* protests. At last the government felt it had to act. Gandhi was arrested at his beach camp on May 5th and tough police action was ordered against the salt campaigners. They continued with their *satyagraha* tactics of non-violent demonstration. But, as usual, Gandhi's arrest led to some violence. In Bengal at least one European was murdered and others wounded. In Chittagong there was a dramatic raid on the Police Armoury. Pathan nationalists known as the Red Shirts seized control of Peshawar, capital of the North West Frontier Province, and held it for four days.

By the middle of the year, nearly 100,000 *satyagraha* campaigners were in jails throughout India. Police had become very free with their *lathis*. They had locked up a large number of women. Once again, the police and government had been made to look unjust and clumsy.

Gandhi with his followers on the Salt March in 1930. He is easily identifiable by his distinctive appearance of homespun dhoti *(loincloth), glasses and shaven head.*

9
The Round Table Conferences

In May 1929 a general election was held in Britain. It was a three-way contest between the Conservatives, the outgoing government led by Stanley Baldwin, the Labour party led by Ramsay MacDonald, and the Liberals under David Lloyd George. The result was Labour 288 seats, Conservatives 260 and Liberals 59.

The new Labour government led by the Prime Minister Ramsay MacDonald instructed the Viceroy in India, Lord Irwin, to make a public promise of full Dominion status for India without waiting for the report of the Simon Commission. This report came out the following year, in June 1930. It did not go as far as recommending Dominion status but it did suggest that the provincial governments should be given more power to work out ways of preparing for this. The Simon Commission proposed that discussions be opened between the British government, delegates from British India and the Indian Princes. Ramsay MacDonald was enthusiastic and a conference was organised to start in London in November. To give it the sound of a discussion among equals it was to be called a 'Round Table Conference'.

The three conferences

The 1930s in Britain were the Depression years, with unemployment rising and tough choices to be made by governments. In the summer of 1931 the Labour government collapsed under the pressure. Ramsay MacDonald agreed to lead a government, with Conservative support, which led to the coalition National Government of 1931.

The first conference

The first Round Table Conference took place from November 1930 to January 1931 in London. Around the table with British officials sat fifty-eight leaders of the Muslim, Hindu and other communities in British India and sixteen from the Princely states. All major Indian groups were represented with one important exception. There was nobody from the Indian National Congress.

It was no surprise that Congress did not take part in November 1930. The campaign in India against the Salt Acts was only just dying down. Gandhi was still in jail. The India Office went ahead with the Round Table Conference partly to show that political gain for India was more likely to come from talking in London than campaigning in Lahore. Their intention was to isolate Congress.

This first conference was a modest success. The Indian Princes agreed to the idea of a self-governing federal British India. The British government agreed to grant full powers to the elected Councils in the provinces and a gradual transfer of power to Indians in the central government of India. No agreement was reached on the communal question, ways of giving guarantees to India's Muslim minority. Hindu and Muslim delegates at the conference made some progress on this but pressures from people in their communities were too strong to achieve a great deal.

Gandhi-Irwin Pact

The India Office now used this modest progress as a bait to tempt Congress. Gandhi and other Congress leaders were released from jail in January 1931. He was invited to talk to the Viceroy, Lord Irwin. After several weeks of discussion Gandhi agreed to stop the civil disobedience campaign and to support the idea of Congress taking part in a second Round Table Conference. Lord Irwin in turn agreed to release all civil disobedience prisoners and to allow picketing of the sale of non-Indian cloth. He also made concessions on salt manufacture on the coast.

The second conference

This agreement, known as the Gandhi-Irwin Pact, was made public in March. Gandhi attended the second Round Table Conference held in London between September and December 1931. He showed little interest in conference discussions and as he was the only Congress representative, nothing much was achieved. The communal question now became more complicated when demands were made on behalf of those outside the Hindu caste system – the 'Untouchables'. The matter was left for a decision by Ramsay MacDonald.

The third conference

Gandhi returned to India in December. No Congress delegates came to the third Round Table Conference in 1932 which achieved even less than the second one. As the Round Table was packed away for the last time in 1932, officials of the India Office felt they had some cause for satisfaction. They believed that the conferences had demonstrated to India and to the world that the British took India seriously, and that all parties in India, even the Indian Congress, had been given a chance to state their case.

The officials now had the job of preparing the drafts for the Government of India Act which British MPs would debate. Through 1933–34 a committee of MPs and numerous civil servants worked out the details. It was all included in the Government of India Act, 1935, the longest-ever piece of law on the Statute book.

The second Round Table Conference, 1931. Why do you think the Conferences were held in England? Do you think this was appropriate?

The Indian Princes

Representatives of the Princes of India came to London to the Round Table Conference in 1930 confident of their position. They were very conservative in government, trying to find a way of keeping their feudal rule over their states in a changing world. Between them they occupied two fifths of India and ruled over some 80 million subjects, over a fifth of the population. Of the 562 Princely states, well over half were very small and of little political importance. At the other end of the scale were great states like Hyderabad, Mysore, Baroda, Travancore and Kashmir, with up-to-date administration and large revenues.

The Rajput states in India formed the most numerous group and were Hindu by religion, as were the Maratha states in the west and Mysore with other states in the south. A group of Sikh states was situated in the Punjab. But in Kashmir a Hindu Prince ruled a mainly Muslim people, while the Hindu majority in states like Hyderabad and Bhopal were ruled by Muslims.

Whatever their size or religion, these states had a common political aim to preserve their position in India. The idea of self-government for

British India raised this question of their status in an urgent form. During the 1920s the Princes' political influence in Indian affairs had been allowed to grow. This was in part because of their enthusiastic support during the First World War. In any case, the British officials had always regarded the Princes as the natural leaders of India, a loyal, conservative balance to the Indian nationalists.

The Chamber of Princes

In 1920 the British government set up the Chamber of Princes in India. All the leading Princes were members and the smaller states elected a few representatives between them. The government of India made a point of talking to the Chamber about India's future. The Princes used it to ask the question 'Who really rules in the states?' The official answer was usually that it was the Princes acting on behalf of the British Crown, but the sixteen Princes who went to London in 1930 for the Round Table Conference were keen to get a federal plan for a future self-governing India. If the British left India they wanted to keep the same local powers. They wanted to be sure that in an independent India the separate states were not dominated by a single central government.

Gandhi in Britain

At the end of August 1931, Gandhi set off for London by sea to attend the second Round Table Conference (see page 45). Also in the party were Gandhi's son Devadas and the Indian industrialist G. D. Birla.

Gandhi was going to London as the only Congress delegate although the British government had hoped for twenty. So many others had wanted to go that it seemed easier to send only one. In any case, many Congress leaders, especially Jawaharlal Nehru, were not at all happy with the Gandhi-Irwin Pact, which seemed to them to offer Congress very little in exchange for calling off civil disobedience. In January Gandhi thought something might be gained by attending the Round Table Conference but even he was not so sure by August. 'There is every chance of my returning empty-handed,' he said as he boarded the ship.

Gandhi quickly lost interest in the conference itself. The India Office, he felt, made too much of the communal issue as an excuse for hanging on to power in India. Devadas Gandhi wrote to Nehru at the start of October about how his father, 'Bapu', was getting on at the conference:

'The whole discussion was sordid... Bapu was pained beyond measure. The opposition was worse than he expected. He has no heart in the work of the Minorities Committee, where MacDonald is as supercilious and patronising as ever.... The informal Committee will meet again tomorrow with Bapu as Chairman, although he is very unhappy in the position and feels that he has been deliberately saddled with the responsibility with a view to discrediting him when the whole thing ultimately fails, as it is bound to do . . . . Before this reaches you the news of the deadlock or the breakdown, which Bapu expects, will already have reached India.'

Gandhi felt that much more could be gained away from the conference being held in St James's Palace. He attracted a lot of media attention and became a celebrity. He chose to stay at Kingsley Hall in the East End of London. He cut an unusual figure walking around the mean local streets in his loincloth, shawl and sandals. He went to tea at Buckingham Palace with King George V dressed like this. Asked afterwards whether he had enough clothes on for such an occasion he replied, 'The King had enough on for both of us!'

He met the comedian Charlie Chaplin, the East End's most famous son, and the playwright George Bernard Shaw, who called himself 'Mahatma Minor' for the occasion. There were many others, only Winston Churchill refusing to see him. He visited Oxford and also Cambridge where the University was developing links with India's political leaders.

Gandhi in the East End of London in September 1931 on his way to meet Charlie Chaplin. The amount of interest he generated is apparent from the crowds who gathered to see him.

Gandhi left London early in December 1931 to return to India. He had obtained good publicity for Congress but the Round Table Conference itself brought the nationalist cause no political gains. Louis Fischer, the American writer and biographer of Gandhi, wrote in 1950 that 'The Round Table Conference was worse than a failure. By intensifying the religious divisions of India it exercised a sinister, tragic influence on the future.'

The Government of India Act, 1935

This long Act, so many years in the making, became law in August 1935. It was an attempt to design a new constitution for India based on the Simon Report and on the three Round Table Conferences. It was a huge compromise, full of checks and balances. The various parties were to be given just enough to keep them happy without giving too much offence to any other group. It was a civil servant's dream but a politician's nightmare.

For the Provinces it did away with dyarchy (see page 27) and gave very full powers to locally elected Councils. This part of the Act took effect in India in 1937. At the centre it laid down a federal structure, bringing together British India and the Princely states. The Princes were to have enough seats in the Federal Legislature (parliament) to give them a powerful position in the new state. The question of communal electorates had been left to Ramsay MacDonald to decide. His 'communal award' of 1932 kept separate electorates for Muslims. It also reserved seats for the Untouchables, a decision which enraged Gandhi, who wanted to abolish the distinction between the Untouchables and the rest of Hindu society.

In fact the federal part of the Act never came into force. In 1935 the British government lacked the political will and economic strength to act in a decisive way over India. Opposition from the Princes and from a few Conservatives led by Winston Churchill delayed things until the outbreak of war in 1939 swept such plans away. The Act had nothing to say about full independence for India, now or in the near future. There was a general understanding that this would come in time, and ten years was sometimes spoken of, but Congress could not be satisfied with this.

10

New nations

New Delhi, the spacious new capital of British India, was designed by the British architect Sir Edwin Lutyens. The buildings were finished by 1930 and were used by the Viceroy and his staff. Around the door of one is written this message:

LIBERTY WILL NOT DESCEND TO A PEOPLE. A PEOPLE MUST RAISE THEM-SELVES TO LIBERTY. IT IS A BLESSING THAT MUST BE EARNED BEFORE IT CAN BE ENJOYED.

This message and the buildings themselves – imposing and expensive – did not suggest that the British government was really in any sort of hurry to hand over ultimate power in India to Indians. Britain's reluctance to allow Indians the blessings of liberty was very clear to the two up-and-coming leaders of the Indian National Congress, Jawaharlal Nehru and Subhas Chandra Bose.

Jawaharlal Nehru

By the time that Jawaharlal Nehru was born in 1889, the family was very well established. His father Motilal Nehru had moved to the city of Allahabad and had become a successful and wealthy lawyer there. As the only son, Jawaharlal had a privileged childhood. Nothing but the best would do. Cheap caps and simple homespun clothes were not part of his wardrobe. He had a series of private English teachers before he was sent to Harrow, an English public school near London, at the age of fifteen. He went on to Cambridge University two years later and after that he studied law in London. He returned to India in 1912 after seven years in England to join his father as a lawyer in Allahabad.

His father, Motilal, was a powerful personality. He was not only a successful lawyer but also an important nationalist politician. He had earned a reputation throughout India as the leading Moderate in the Indian National Congress, and he was keen that his son Jawaharlal should have a chance to become an important politician as well.

Nehru campaigning

Jawaharlal Nehru began to speak at meetings of Congress but his first big chance to shine came in 1920. In that year Gandhi launched the non-cooperation campaign against the British (see page 40). Nehru threw himself into the campaign with great energy. He made many tours to remote village areas and for the first time he came to see the problems of ordinary Indians for himself. He organised volunteers and made many speeches. In his autobiography he later described the effect that village India had on him and his fellow campaigners:

> 'Enormous gatherings would take place at the briefest notice by word of mouth. One village would communicate with another, and the second with the third and so on, and presently whole villages would empty out and, all over the fields there would be men and women and children on the march to the meeting place.... They were in miserable rags, men and women, but their faces were full of excitement and their eyes glistened and seemed to expect strange happenings which would, as if by a miracle, put an end to their long misery... I was filled with shame and sorrow, shame at my own easy going and comfortable life and our petty politics of the city which ignored this vast multitude of semi-naked sons and daughters of India, sorrow at the degredation and overwhelming poverty of India.'

> J. Nehru, *An Autobiography*, 1936.

The village campaign brought Nehru closer to the masses of village India and showed him that he had the skill and power to bring them into his political work. He later wrote that he 'experienced the thrill of mass feeling, the power of influencing the mass'. That power led him into conflict with the British who arrested Nehru and put him in jail.

It was the first of nine jail sentences that he served between 1921 and 1942. They added up to just over nine years of his life but each one strengthened the nationalist movement and his position as one of its most important and best-known leaders. From Nehru's point of view, each arrest was another blow at the right of Britain to rule his country.

Political ideas

Gandhi abandoned non-cooperation in 1922 while Nehru was still in jail. From that time, Nehru began to work out his own approach to India's problems. He was attracted by the ideas of socialism, especially after a short visit to Europe in 1926. He visited the USSR where he was impressed with the efforts of the Soviet leaders to overcome the agricultural and industrial backwardness of their country. He began to see India's struggle for independence as part of a worldwide movement shared by other nations trying to break free from colonial rule. He demanded that Congress press for full independence rather than the Dominion status which his father and other Moderates wanted. Nehru had the support of the younger Congress leaders including Subhas Chandra Bose. Gandhi wanted to avoid a split in Congress and used his influence to get Nehru elected as President of Congress just before the start of the second civil disobedience campaign in 1930 (see page 42).

Nehru had little interest in the Round Table Conferences because he thought the discussions irrelevant to India's needs. President of Congress again in 1936, he made his own views very clear.

'I see no way of ending the poverty, the vast unemployment, the degradation, and the subjection of the Indian people except through Socialism.... It means ultimately a change in our instincts, habits and desires. In short it means a new civilisation, radically different from the present capitalist order. Some glimpse we can have of this new civilisation in the territories of the USSR. Much has happened there which has pained me greatly and with which I disagree but I look upon that great and fascinating unfolding of a new order and a new civilisation as the most promising feature of our dismal age.... I do not know how or when this new order will come to India....'

Subhas Chandra Bose

Subhas Chandra Bose was the sixth son and ninth child of a successful Bengali lawyer from Orissa. Born in 1897 he was a clever pupil who did well at school. His parents also insisted that he learn Sanskrit, the language of the ancient Hindu writings. His interest in Hinduism grew and as a student at Calcutta University he became an admirer of Aurobindo Ghose, the Hindu nationalist from Bengal. His student years were those of the First World War and Bose found some aspects of military life attractive. He joined the Calcutta University unit of the India Defence Force.

Bose was sent to Cambridge University by his father in 1919 to prepare for the entry examination into the ICS (see page 14). He passed with high marks and gained a place in the ICS but a few months later he resigned. He returned to India to take part in the non-cooperation movement which had just started under Gandhi's leadership. This, he felt, was where he really belonged.

Bose began to take a leading part in Congress at the same time as Jawaharlal Nehru. Like Nehru he was given his start and pushed forward by a leading Congress figure, Chittaranjan Das, the leading nationalist in Bengal. Bose shared Nehru's interest in socialism and in getting young people involved in the nationalist movement. He joined Nehru in pressing for full Independence.

During the 1920s Bose began to move away from Gandhi. He had never shared many of Gandhi's ideas, any more than had Nehru, but now he began to doubt whether Gandhi was a suitable leader of Congress as well. He told a student audience that those who lived in ashrams would always be respected in India,

'But it is not their lead we shall have to follow if we are to create a new India at once free, happy and great.... When India is free she will have to fight her modern enemies with modern methods, both in the economic and in the political spheres. The days of the bullock cart are gone and gone forever.'

'A politician trying to be a saint'

This was Gandhi's reply when he was asked if he was a saint trying to be a politician. A very moral man he certainly was, a saintly man he may have been. But he was also the son and grandson of Chief Ministers, men who had learned political survival in the turbulent world of Kathiawar politics.

Gandhi and Nehru

Gandhi showed his political skill in the way that he outmanoeuvred Bose, who tried to take over the leadership of the Indian National Congress during the 1930s. Gandhi used his own influence within the party to push forward the only other possible candidate, Jawaharlal Nehru, although he was not entirely happy about Nehru's leadership either. He wrote to an English friend in 1936:

> 'Jawaharlal's way is not my way. I accept his ideal about land, etc. But I do not accept practically any of his methods. I would strain every nerve to prevent a class war. So would he, I expect. But he does not believe it to be possible to avoid it. I believe it to be perfectly possible especially if my method is accepted. But though Jawaharlal is extreme in his presentation of his methods, he is sober in action.'

In Gandhi's opinion, Subhas Chandra Bose was likely to support violence. Moreover, despite their differences, Gandhi liked Nehru a lot. He felt close to him in spirit and Nehru felt the same about Gandhi.

For these reasons, Gandhi worked to have Nehru elected as President of Congress in 1936. This was a vital year because the party was getting ready for the elections the following year to the Provincial governments under the 1935 Government of India Act (see page 49). Nehru stormed around the campaign trail with great energy. Over 30 million Indians were entitled to vote in these elections. In eight months from May 1936, he spoke to about 10 million of them in countless meetings up and down the country.

The 1937 elections

Nehru's election tour was a great success. Not only did it make certain that Nehru would follow Gandhi as Congress leader but it helped the party to a surprise victory when the votes of the 1937 elections were counted. Congress gained a clear majority in six of the eleven provinces of British India. In three of the remaining five provinces it became the single biggest party.

It was the promise of separate electorates which brought Mohammad Ali Jinnah (see page 25) back to India. He had dropped out of politics in 1932 and settled in London. In 1935 he returned to India convinced that he could achieve great things for Indian Muslims.

The Muslim vote

As President of the Muslim League he worked hard to get the party

Nehru addressing a public meeting in a village in 1937. Overall he made speeches to over 10 million people. He later described the distance he covered, mostly in rural areas; it was 'about 26,000 miles by railway, 22,500 by road (chiefly by car) and 1,600 by air. The means of transport varied greatly, they included aeroplanes, railway (usually third class railway, sometimes second class . . .) motor cars . . . motor lorry, horse carriage, tonga, ekka, bullock cart, bicycle, elephant, camel, horse, steamer, paddle boat, canoe and on foot.'

into shape for the 1937 elections. The results were a bitter disappointment. He had expected Congress to do well in the eight Hindu majority provinces but he expected the Muslim League to win most seats in the four Muslim majority provinces. In fact Congress became the biggest party in two of these, Bengal and Assam. Even in Punjab and Sind it was not the Muslim League which profited from the defeat of Congress. Punjab went to the Unionist Party and in Sind the Muslim vote split four ways. For Jinnah it was a great set-back.

The best that the Muslim League could now hope for was some sort of deal with Congress for a share in the governments of some provinces. Jinnah pushed hard for this but in the end Congress refused to share power in this way. The Congress leaders felt that the election results proved that Indians no longer saw the need to protect the political rights of communities. Many Muslims had in fact voted for Congress and even in Muslim areas the League had not done well. Congress, they said, was now the only party for Indian nationalists of all communities.

The two nations

Jinnah was not the man to accept the collapse of the Muslim League without a fight. The party was re-organised, with paid party officials, a membership fee low enough to suit even the poorest Muslim, and party branches in even the smallest villages. But his most effective policy was to try to show that Congress did not, as Nehru had claimed, represent the wishes of India's Muslims. The Muslim League alone did that, argued Jinnah. Pressing this argument was bound to increase tensions between Muslims and Hindus. The League published allegations about the mistreatment of Muslims in Hindu majority areas.

Jinnah and the Muslim League

Jinnah's speech at the League's 1938 Conference gives the flavour of the disputes:

> 'The Congress leaders may shout as much as they like that the Congress is a national body. But I say it is not true. The Congress is nothing but a Hindu body. That is the truth and the Congress leaders know it. The presence of a few Muslims, the few misled and misguided ones, and the few who are there with ulterior motives does not, cannot, make it a national body. I challenge anybody to deny that the Congress is not mainly a Hindu body.
>
> I ask does the Congress represent the Muslim? (Shouts of 'No, no')
> I ask does the Congress represent the Christians? ('No')
> I ask does the Congress represent the Scheduled Castes? ('No')
> I ask does the Congress represent the non-Brahmins? ('No')
> I say the Congress does not even represent all the Hindus!'

This was Jinnah's line at the big political meetings. He was also coming to accept the view that the Muslim League should aim for a separate state for Muslims. The idea had first been suggested at a political meeting of Muslims in 1930. Three years later an Indian Muslim student at Cambridge University, Rahmat Ali, wrote a pamphlet supporting the idea. He even invented a name for this Muslim state – PAKISTAN. The word itself means 'Land of the Pure' in Urdu and it is made up in this way:

P from Punjab
A from Afghania (his name for the North West Frontier Province)
K from Kashmir
s from Sind
TAN from Baluchistan

The I between K and S does not come into the word when written in Urdu.

At the time Rahmat Ali's ideas were not taken very seriously by politicians in India but the 1937 elections had changed that.

Jinnah was becoming convinced that only in a Muslim state could Islamic Law guide the daily lives of Muslims. Neither a Hindu-dominated India nor Nehru's socialism could offer that.

Jinnah's campaign to revive the Muslim League was a success. Many Muslims joined the party and Muslim leaders in Punjab and Bengal at last joined the League. By 1939 Jinnah had become a much more powerful figure in Indian politics and the leaders of Congress now wanted talks with him. Jinnah would not speak to Congress. Things were still going his way.

In March 1940, at the League Conference in Lahore, the party took the formal decision to insist on a separate Muslim state when Independence came to India. This Lahore Resolution gave Muslim League backing to the idea of Pakistan, an idea hardly taken seriously by anyone only ten years before. In his speech at Lahore, Jinnah denied that there had ever been one nation in India:

'The present artificial unity of India dates back only to the British conquest and is maintained by the British bayonet....'

Jinnah photographed in 1926

11
War 1939–45

Congress and the war

Britain and France declared war on Germany on 3rd September, 1939. In India Lord Linlithgow, the Viceroy, announced that India too was at war with Germany. There was no discussion with Indian political leaders. Congress, with governments in most of the Provinces, was especially angry about this lack of consultation. The 1935 India Act had not yet come into effect fully (see page 49) so Linlithgow's decision was strictly speaking legal, but bad politics.

Nehru had been in China when war was declared. He hurried back to India keen both to join the fight against fascism and to continue his struggle for freedom from British rule. These two causes were linked in Nehru's mind but they caused a practical problem for him and for Congress. Was there a policy that would do both things, help Britain and her allies defeat fascism as well as get the British to leave India as soon as possible?

Congress resigns

After a lot of discussion Congress made an offer to the government of India: they would support the British in the war in exchange for a promise that India would get Independence soon after the end of the war; during the war Indians should be included in the central government of India and given real political power. Linlithgow was not interested in this offer from Congress. He felt certain enough of support from other political groups in India. Nehru asked Jinnah to join him in protest but without success and at the end of October all the Congress governments in the provinces resigned. They were run by their British Governors for the rest of the war.

In the summer of 1940 the war in Europe took a bad turn for Britain and her Allies. Germany invaded Belgium and Holland in May and a British army had to be evacuated from Dunkirk. Italy joined Germany on what it now assumed was the winning side. Britain had a new Prime Minister, Winston Churchill, and a new Secretary of State for India – but the same old policy for India. Gandhi and Nehru wanted to support Britain but Linlithgow's vague promises of Dominion status for India some time after the war were not nearly enough. Most in Congress no longer trusted British intentions. Linlithgow seemed to them to be favouring Jinnah and his Two Nation theory (see page 54). For their part the British were still not convinced that Congress really did speak for Indians from all communities, as it claimed to do. They also thought Congress was trying to take advantage of Britain's military crisis.

Satyagraha

Congress reacted with campaigns of civil disobedience. Gandhi led a *satyagraha* campaign starting in October 1940. By the end of 1941 some 30,000 nationalists had been jailed but by then the military situation had become even worse for the Allies.

In June 1941 German armies invaded the USSR and in December the Japanese attacked the main US naval base in the Pacific at Pearl Harbor, Hawaii. The war had now become truly world-wide and the defence of India was even more vital to Britain and the Allies. She was an important base for protecting Middle Eastern oil fields to the west and resisting the Japanese advance in the east. In India all Congress prisoners were released from jail but in February 1942 Britain's reputation in Asia had its biggest blow with the Japanese capture of Singapore and the surrender of 80,000 British, Indian and Australian troops to a Japanese army less than half its size.

The Home Front

Congress did nothing to support the war effort directly and the Muslim League gave only cautious support, but individual Indians joined the army on a large scale. A peacetime force of some 200,000 men, mainly frontier units, became a huge modern army of 2½ million men, the largest volunteer army in the world. These men had to be trained and provided with equipment which gave an enormous boost to industry in India. During the 1930s the army had made the change from horse-drawn vehicles and cavalry to lorries and tanks. Many of the young men who joined this mechanised army came out with a useful education and training.

Following the capture of Singapore, the Japanese went on to drive out British and American troops from Burma by May 1942. Japanese forces were now on India's north-eastern border. Calcutta was bombed and Japanese warships cruised in the Bay of Bengal. In Calcutta the British organised some civil defence with air raid wardens but many Indians had mixed feelings. The Japanese declared their huge empire the 'Greater Asia Co-Prosperity Sphere', a title suggesting partnership. It was nothing of the sort, but for some Indian nationalists the sight of an Asian power driving out European imperialists was a cheering one.

The loss of Burma had another important effect. Burmese rice had been an important source of food in Bengal but now this was lost. This, with cyclones, floods and a feeble government response, gave rise to a terrible famine in Bengal in 1943 and 1944. It is estimated that perhaps 2 million Bengalis died as a result.

The Cripps Mission, 1942

Stafford Cripps was a British socialist MP who had been expelled from the Labour Party in 1939 for his extreme views. Despite this, Churchill noticed his ability and sent him as ambassador to the USSR. Cripps returned from Moscow claiming the credit for bringing the USSR into the war, a hero to left-wing opinion in Britain. Cripps was becoming too popular for Churchill's liking but the war was going badly and he needed the support of the left. In February 1942 Churchill re-organised his war cabinet, making Cripps leader of the House of Commons.

In India the military situation looked very bad. In London it was thought that a full-scale Japanese invasion of India was likely. Churchill needed a deal with Congress for their full support in the war effort, despite his dislike of the Indian nationalists. The United States and China, Britain's main allies in the front line against the Japanese, were also very keen that some deal be made by the British government with the various Indian political groups. Churchill decided to send Cripps, who by now had a popular reputation as a diplomat and was on good terms with many Congress leaders. It was suggested by some that Churchill wanted a political rival out of the way on a difficult mission, but historians have shown that Cripps agreed with the terms of the mission. He flew to India in March 1942.

The Cripps Plan

Although Churchill was under pressure, the plan he told Cripps to offer Indian leaders was just not attractive enough, especially to Congress. As soon as the war was over, under the plan Britain offered, elections would be held to allow Indians to elect an assembly that would have the power to decide on a constitution for a self-governing Dominion of India. Any Province that did not want to join this Indian Union was to be allowed to go its own way and become a separate Dominion. This was called at the time the 'Pakistan Option' because it seemed to support the idea of a separate Muslim state. The Cripps plan also seemed to give the Indian Princes the chance to keep their independence as rulers. Congress did not see the future of India in this way at all.

The other main problem was what sort of government should rule in India while the war continued. Congress demanded a National government free from British control. Britain, and to some extent the USA, feared that such a government might make a separate peace with Japan.

The Cripps Plan had been drawn up in London. The Viceroy and government of India, who had not been consulted, were annoyed by this and by the fact that Colonel Johnson, President Roosevelt's special envoy to India, had been invited to take an active part in the talks. The Cripps Plan therefore failed to win the whole-hearted support of the British in India. It was also being turned down by Congress. Cripps returned to London empty-handed.

President Roosevelt wrote Churchill a private letter asking that Cripps be kept on in India to make a last effort to reach a deal. The

Stafford Cripps (left) with Jinnah during his visit to India.

President wrote that people in the USA just did not understand why Britain would not give India self-government now if they would do so after the war.

Churchill did not want to fall out with Roosevelt but replied that he could not risk the defence of India in this way. At least he could say to the Americans that he had tried.

'Quit India'

After the failure of the Cripps Mission, Congress took its lead from Gandhi who was now sure that the British no longer had the right to rule in India. The very real threat of a Japanese invasion of India made this the ideal time to tell the British to 'Quit India'.

Congress made a formal demand that Britain should pull out of India immediately at a meeting in Bombay on 8th August 1942. If the British refused, Congress threatened a major campaign of civil disobedience. It was Nehru who put the resolution to Congress saying, 'We are now taking a step from which there will be no going back.... It is going to be a fight to the finish. The Congress has now burnt its boats and is about to embark upon a desperate campaign.'

Gandhi's mood was just as determined when he explained to journalists what Congress had agreed. 'This is open rebellion' he told them, and wrote:

'There are powerful elements of fascism in British rule and in India these are the elements which we see and feel every day. If the British wish...to win the war and make the world better, they must purify themselves by surrendering power in India.'

Congress leaders in jail

The British response was all too predictable. On the day after the 'Quit India' demand, Gandhi, Nehru and all the other Congress leaders were arrested in Bombay. The government of India felt that it could not tolerate a civil disobedience campaign when India was threatened with invasion. With all their leaders in jail, the nationalist protests were certain to be uncontrolled, and violent.

The worst troubles came when local nationalist groups managed to cut rail and communication lines with the armies fighting the Japanese in the north-east. Local officials often lost control as crowds attacked government offices, police stations and railways. Special groups of armed police were rushed to these areas to restore order. The standing orders were never to fire warning shots in the air because a rioting crowd might think the police had missed, encouraging them to attack and overwhelm the police. Police orders were to shoot to kill from the start. Casualty figures rose sharply.

In Bihar, two RAF officers were killed on a train between Calcutta and Delhi. An Anglo-Indian officer of the Provincial Service was tied to his office chair, drenched with kerosene and burned to death. In Patna, the State capital, the Governor was besieged in Government House for weeks. He was rescued eventually by troops but it took another six months to regain full control there.

Damage to the railway in Bihar had been extensive. Engines had been de-railed and sections of track removed. The main line through Patna was out of action for a while and was not fully repaired for months. British anger about the mob violence and the Bihar murders led them to use excessive force to regain control in some places. A District Officer in south-west Bihar wrote to a friend about the troubles in his area. 'We also had a visit from the Military Police, Punjabis who don't care much for Biharis at the best of times, who burnt two or three villages near where the railway line had been damaged, and shot all the inhabitants who ran away.'

It has been estimated that by the end of the year nearly 1,000 people had been killed and 60,000 arrested.

The Indian Army at war

All of this political activity in India during the war had very little effect on the activities of the Indian Army.

Indian troops were already in Egypt at the outbreak of war in 1939. They formed the basis of the 4th Indian Division, an infantry force who gained the highest reputation in North Africa and later in Italy. The Indian Army never had less than two full divisions in this area despite the military crisis in Burma. Further east other Indian soldiers were sent into action in Iraq and Persia. The Germans had helped local rebels in an effort to gain control of these two countries and their vital oil production.

By far the greatest number of Indian soldiers were involved in the fighting in Malaya and Burma. The Japanese attack on the US Fleet at Pearl Harbor in December 1941 was followed by the capture of the great British military and naval base of Singapore in February 1942. The Japanese had shown an ability to attack through dense jungle which their Indian, British and Australian opponents had not believed possible.

Singapore and Burma

British military planners had thought Singapore could not be attacked by land. They were wrong. They had thought that Burma, surrounded by mountains to the north, west and east, could only be invaded as the British themselves had done, from the south and by sea. British confidence in her own superior naval power led them to assume that the defence of Burma was secure. The planners were wrong again and in the first half of 1942 the Imperial Japanese Army took full advantage. They drove north into Burma, pushing back an outnumbered and ill-equipped Allied force, quite untrained for jungle warfare. In March the Japanese captured Rangoon, the Burmese capital, and in May the British and Indian troops who had survived the long retreat entered India. General Slim, their commander, wrote about the coming of the monsoon rains on 12th May:

'From then on the retreat was sheer misery. Ploughing their way up slopes, over a track inches deep in slippery mud, soaked to the skin, rotten with fever, ill fed and shivering as the air grew cooler, the troops went on, hour after hour, day after day. Their only rest at night was to lie on the sodden ground under the dripping trees, without even a blanket to cover them. On the last day of that nine hundred-mile retreat I watched the rearguard march into India. All of them, British, Indian and Gurkha, were gaunt and ragged as scarecrows. Yet they still carried their arms and kept their ranks, they were still recognizable as fighting units.'

General Slim's memoirs are called *Defeat into Victory* but it was a slow process. In the summer of 1942 the monsoon rains stopped all military activity and the Indian Army re-grouped. The Japanese Navy came into the Bay of Bengal in strength and carrier-borne aircraft bombed targets along India's east coast. A hundred ships were sunk. The small Royal Indian Navy could offer little resistance.

Counter-attack in Burma

During 1943 units of the Indian 14th Army, commanded by Slim, began to counter-attack against the Japanese but without much success at first. However, supplies, training and morale were improving fast. In March 1944 came the decisive battle of Imphal, where five Japanese divisions launching an attack on India were checked by the 17th and 21st Indian Divisions. Large reinforcements arrived for the Indian Army but fierce fighting continued for months. Not until June did the Japanese, starving and exhausted, begin to fall back. For the last year of the war the Japanese were pushed, grimly resisting, back through Burma. Of the twenty-four Victoria Crosses won in Burma, twenty went to the Indian Army.

Bose and the Indian National Army

Subhas Chandra Bose resigned from Congress in 1939 after falling out with Gandhi and Nehru. He still had a large number of supporters, especially in his home province of Bengal. Since the mid-1930s Bose had been attracted by the ideas of the fascists in Europe. He admired the Italian dictator Mussolini and hoped to adapt some fascist ideas to Indian conditions. He made no secret of his wish to drive the British out of India by any means. When war broke out in September 1939 the government of India kept a very close watch on his activities, believing him to be dangerous. Bose was arrested many times and by January 1941 he was released from prison for the eleventh time. He made a dramatic escape from house arrest, slipping into Afghanistan disguised as a deaf-mute Muslim camel driver. From there he travelled to Berlin and called on Hitler to ask for support. His plan was to form an Indian National Army from captured Indian prisoners of war, to fight against the British and help drive them out of India.

Formation of the INA

In 1943 Bose was sent by German submarine and Japanese aeroplane to Japan. General Tojo, the Japanese leader, gave him a warm welcome there and the Indian National Army (INA) was formed in Singapore, a force of some 15,000 men. Bose was declared 'Supreme Commander' of this make-shift army but his friends and followers called him 'Netaji', the 'Leader'.

Most INA recruits had been captured after the fall of Singapore and put under pressure by the Japanese. They were never used by the Japanese as front line troops. After the defeat of the Japanese at Imphal, the morale of the INA suffered. Desertions increased and the entire 1st Division of the INA, 3,000 men, surrendered. As Slim noted later, 'our Indian and Gurkha troops were at times not too ready to let them surrender and orders had to be issued to give them a kinder welcome.'

Bose himself died in a plane crash in August 1945 on the island of Taiwan. Soldiers of the Indian National Army who surrendered or were captured were technically guilty of treason in wartime but Bose did not accept Britain's right to rule in India and called himself the Head of State of Azad Hind, Free India. The very existence of the INA had been kept secret by the British but by the summer of 1945 some decision had to be taken.

It was clear to all that India's independence was coming soon. More and more nationalist politicians were coming publicly to the defence of the INA men whom the British wanted to put on trial. In the end just three officers were dismissed from the Army but were given no other punishment. The nationalist tide in India was running more strongly every day and that included the Indian Army. It was a time to look forward, not back.

12

The Transfer of Power

By the spring of 1945 it was clear that the war was in its last few months. In India the public mood was rising fast in the certainty that Britain would transfer power. Almost all Indians were nationalists now. This applied to the officers and men of the Indian Army who had fought for freedom in their own way by their outstanding contribution to the Allied war effort. It also applied to Congress who had refused to co-operate during the war and even to the Indian National Army, now nationalist heroes to some, who had put their faith in Japan.

Wavell in India

In Britain, too, public opinion was clearly in favour of a rapid transfer of power in India. Lord Wavell, the army general appointed by Churchill as Viceroy in India in 1944, was called back to London in March 1945. When he returned to India two months later it was with orders to release Nehru and other Congress leaders from jail, where they had been detained without trial since 1942, and to call the political leaders of all parties to a conference. It took place in Simla, the graceful summer retreat of the government of India in the hills north-west of Delhi. Wavell offered the politicians the chance to form a Viceroy's Council, which would be the government of India, with the task of organising the transfer of power from Britain. The only British members would be the Viceroy himself and the Commander-in-Chief. In the end the Simla conference failed because Jinnah insisted that all Muslims on this Viceroy's Council were to be chosen by the Muslim League. Congress would not accept this: with a Muslim President and other prominent Muslims among its leaders, it claimed to speak for all Indians. During the Simla conference, the war in Europe came to an end.

The Cabinet Mission

In the general election in Britain at the end of July, a Labour government was elected. Clement Attlee replaced Churchill as Prime Minister. Japan surrendered on 14th August 1945. The new British Labour government was determined to quicken the pace towards independence for India. It announced that there were to be elections for the central and provincial governments and all parties agreed to take part in them. The results showed just how far Jinnah and the Muslim League had gone in convincing Indian Muslims that a separate Muslim state – Pakistan – was the only solution for them. For while almost all non-Muslim seats went to Congress, the Muslim League won almost all Muslim seats. Jinnah was more determined than ever to hold out for a separate Pakistan.

In the months that followed the anti-British mood in the country sharpened, made worse by famine, drought in some areas and widespread acute food shortages. There was rioting and looting in Bombay, Calcutta and Delhi. In Bombay some sailors of the Royal Indian Navy mutinied and only gave up at the request of Congress leaders. There was also popular support for the three Indian National Army men put on trial (see page 63). This, together with the mutiny, especially alarmed the government of India.

Pethwick-Lawrence in India

In March 1946 Lord Pethwick-Lawrence, the new Secretary of State for India, arrived in Delhi at the head of the Cabinet Mission. Also in the group was Sir Stafford Cripps, returning to India four years after the failure of his own attempt to settle the political future of India. The Mission spent weeks in discussions with Indian political leaders from all parties. They stayed in imperial comfort in New Delhi. Gandhi stayed in a simple hut in the poorest part of town among the Harijans, the 'Untouchables'. Thousands attended his daily prayer meetings.

By May the Mission had made no progress at all. Gandhi advised Pethwick-Lawrence to announce a plan for the transfer of power. They proposed a united India with a federal government to deal with foreign affairs, defence and communications, covering both British India and the Princely states. Any decision on an important communal or religious question would have to have a majority from both Hindu and Muslim members.

The Provinces would be grouped with places reserved for the communal groups in the important Constituent Assembly which would decide the new Constitution of India. The Provinces would have a lot of power to decide local issues and could work together in groups on issues common to all.

In suggesting this plan the Cabinet Mission did not accept the idea of a separate Muslim state of Pakistan. Jinnah claimed that Muslims should rule in six Provinces, including all of Punjab, Bengal and Assam. The Cabinet Mission felt that far too many Hindus would be left in such a Muslim state and would cause more communal problems. However, the Muslim League did not want to split Punjab and Bengal. The Cabinet Mission knew very well how difficult such a division would be in practice, which is why they did not believe that a separate Pakistan was possible.

Congress doubts

Gandhi considered that 'it is the best document the British government could have produced in the circumstances'. Congress was not so sure and Nehru and the other leaders went off to Mussoorie in the hills north of Delhi to think about their response. Jinnah did not like it all at first, holding out for a separate Pakistan. In the end he accepted that it was the best he could get at the time. Perhaps he felt that, as the Mission said, it gave the benefits of Pakistan without the problems. The Muslim League accepted early in June.

Congress seemed uncertain and confused. Gandhi now began to have second thoughts about the plan without saying why. Some in Congress feared that the solid block of Muslim votes in some areas would lead to a breakaway from India even though this 'Pakistan option' was not set out in the plan. Most were suspicious of British motives. Cripps and Pethwick-Lawrence went behind the Viceroy's back and suggested that Congress should compromise by accepting the plan while refusing to take part in the transitional government that would rule India while elections were held.

Muslim League rejection

When the All India Congress met in Bombay in early July to consider the compromise, Nehru made a fiery speech in which he said that Congress was only agreeing to go on to discuss a new constitution for India. If it wished, it could scrap all plans for provinces after that. This was too much for Jinnah, already uneasy about having accepted the plan. Indignant at what they saw as Congress double-dealing, the Muslim League now completely rejected the Cabinet Mission plan. Jinnah fixed 16th August, 1946 as Direct Action Day and when that day came he declared,

'What we have done today is the most historic act in our history. Never have we in the whole history of the League done anything except by constitutional methods...but now we are obliged and forced into this position. This day we bid goodbye to constitutional methods.'

The last Viceroy

Viceroy: Mr Nehru, I want you to regard me not as the last Viceroy winding up the British Raj, but as the first to lead the way to the new India.

Nehru: Now I know what they mean when they speak of your charm being so dangerous.

This last Viceroy was Lord Louis Mountbatten, dashing senior naval officer, cousin of King George VI, who had been the Commander-in-Chief of all Allied forces in South-East Asia in the last years of the war. He replaced Lord Wavell who had been called back to Britain after the failure of the Cabinet Mission and the communal violence that followed Jinnah's Direct Action Day in August 1946. The Prime Minister, Clement Attlee, decided that the only policy for India was to set a definite date for the transfer of power to the Indians themselves and to find someone with the personal qualities to get the job done in the best way possible. He chose Mountbatten.

Mountbatten

Mountbatten arrived in Delhi in March 1947. With him came his elegant wife Edwina, his daughter Pamela, a hand-picked group of advisers and the gaggle of newsmen which follows such a glamorous party. Before taking the job, Mountbatten had demanded two things. First he wanted full powers to negotiate in India without interference from London. Second, a promise that after the job was done he could become Britain's First Sea Lord. Attlee personally agreed to both.

In fact the political situation in India was well beyond the personal control of any individual by this time. All the many meetings between Mountbatten and the political leaders of India – Jinnah, Nehru, Patel and others – could not hide the fact that there were few decisions left to make. After the failure of earlier plans, some sort of Partition, splitting India up into two or more parts, was bound to come. It was now a question of deciding the form of Partition and when it should take place.

Partition plan

By early May, Mountbatten thought he had the best answers to these two questions. His partition plan was to transfer power to the six Hindu provinces to form an independent India but to give each of the Muslim or Muslim majority provinces the chance to decide their future. Non-Muslim districts in Punjab and Bengal would have a chance to join India. On the question of timing, Mountbatten wanted to speed up the process. Attlee had sent him to India with June 1948 as the deadline for Independence. As soon as Partition was announced, it would no longer be possible to take the loyalty of Hindu and Muslim civil servants and armed forces for granted as their future would now be in either Pakistan or India. Violence between communities increased every day. The shorter the period of uncertainty the better, he felt, and fixed 15th August, 1947 as the new date for the transfer of power.

Mountbatten had not shown the plan either to Jinnah or Nehru but was confident that both would accept it. He was wrong. Nehru felt the plan would lead to the breakaway from India, not just of Pakistan but also of other independent states. It would lead, said Nehru, to 'chaos and weakness'. The crisis was solved by the advice of V. P. Menon, one of the Viceroy's advisers who had never liked the plan. Menon now suggested the transfer of power to just two states, India and Pakistan, both to have Dominion status as members of the British Commonwealth. The chance of an independent Bengal or Punjab was dropped.

This was the plan formally presented to Indian political leaders in Delhi on 2nd June. Baldev Singh accepted on behalf of the Sikhs. Nehru and Patel accepted on behalf of Congress, provided the Muslim League did also. The following day Jinnah nodded his head on behalf of the League.

Independence days, 1947

The agreed plan for the transfer of power left only two and a half

Lord Mountbatten presides over a staff meeting with an ever-present reminder that time before the hand-over of power was getting shorter.

months in which to make many difficult decisions. The staff and officers of the civil service and the men and equipment of the armed forces had to be divided between Pakistan and India. The assets of British India – railways, canals and institutions of all kinds – had to be shared out as well. Most difficult of all was to decide exactly where the new border was to run between the two new countries, cutting right across Bengal in the north-east and Punjab in the north-west. Two Boundary Commissions were set up. Sir Cyril Radcliffe was chairman of both, working with two Muslim and two Hindu judges. Their task was to decide where the new borders should run but they could not agree.

The Radcliffe Award

Radcliffe had to take the final decision himself. The map shows this decision, known as the Radcliffe Award, but it cannot show the tragic results for families and friends who would find themselves living on different sides of the frontier. There was bound to be a political storm over the Award and for this reason it was not made public until two days after Independence.

As 15th August approached the last big problem to be solved was the future of the Princely states. One hundred million people lived in these states, mostly in Hindu areas. After 15th August their rulers, the Princes, were to be free to choose whether or not to join India or Pakistan, or to become independent. Congress naturally expected almost all of the states to join India but throughout June and July many seemed undecided. Congress offered a tempting deal to persuade the uncertain ones. The states would only have to give up their powers over Defence, Foreign Affairs and Communications to India, powers which the British had always had anyway. Otherwise the Princes could keep all their old powers within their states.

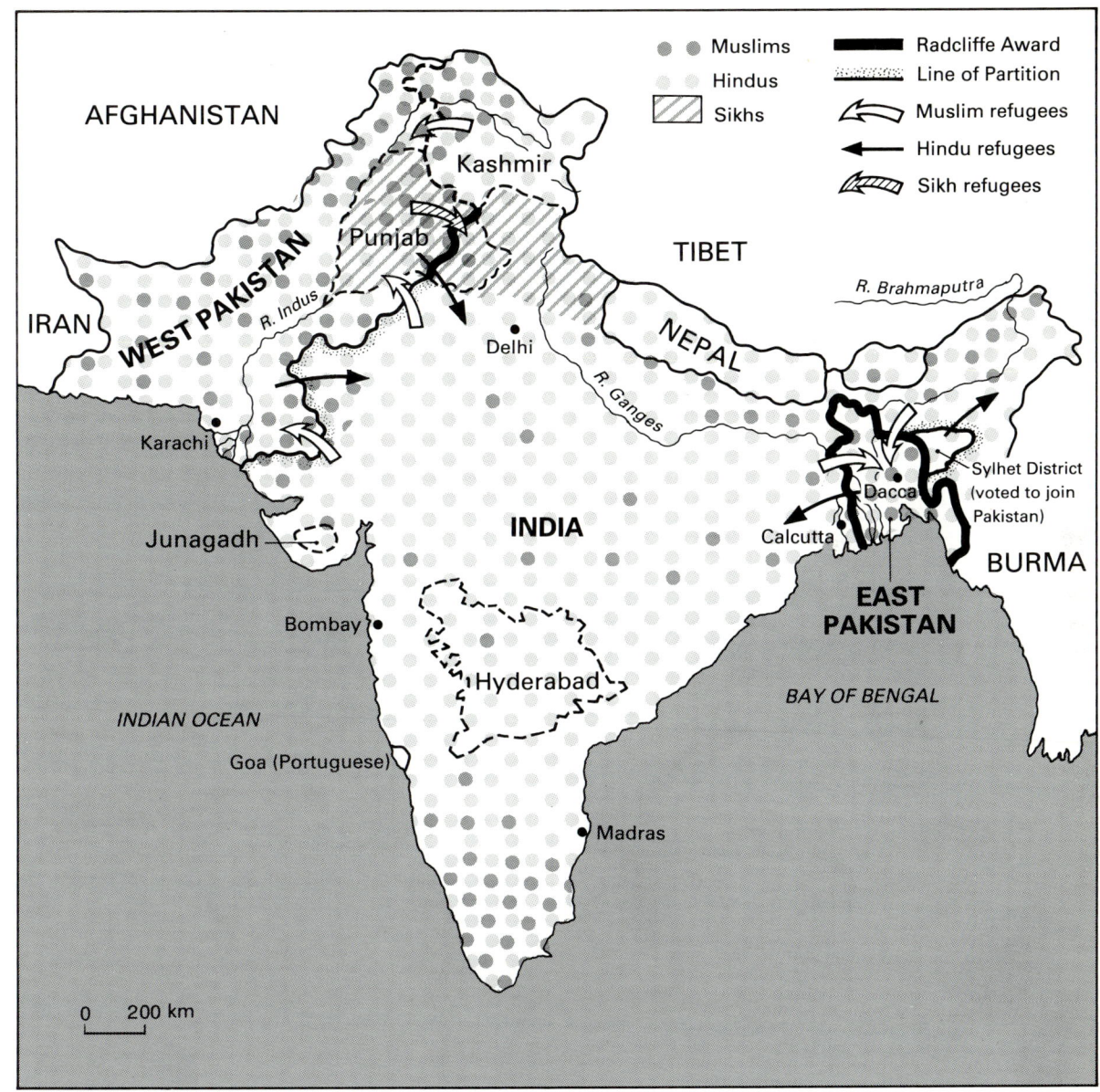

Partition and Independence, 1947.

The Princes

A conference for the Princes was arranged by Congress for the end of July and they asked Mountbatten to help in persuading the Princes to join India. He pointed out to the Princes that they had little hope of a political future if they tried to keep their independence surrounded by new states which were recognised by the world's powers. After the conference the Indian political leaders and Mountbatten kept up the pressure on the Princes to make up their minds. By 15th August all but three had decided they would bring their states into either Pakistan or India. For most the decision was in favour of India because they were

Hindu rulers over Hindu people. For Kashmir, Hyderabad and the tiny state of Junagadh matters were not that simple. The ruler of Kashmir was a Hindu and his people were mostly Muslims. Hyderabad and Junagadh had Muslim rulers and subjects from both faiths. All three tried to buy time by refusing to declare for either state.

Pakistan

On 14th August, 1947 Pakistan became an independent country. Lord Mountbatten flew to its new capital, Karachi, to hand over all powers to Jinnah who became Governor General of the new state. Very few people had taken the idea of a separate Muslim state very seriously until the last difficult years of British India.

In his speech Mountbatten reminded the audience of this fact:

'The birth of Pakistan is an event in history. History seems sometimes to move with the infinite slowness of a glacier, and sometimes to rush forward in a torrent. Just now, in this part of the world, our united efforts have melted the ice . . . and we are carried in the full flood. There is not time to look back. There is only time to look forward.'

Jinnah being sworn-in as Governor General of Pakistan. He is shown standing on the platform on the left of the picture, next to the Chief Justice.

India: freedom at midnight

That same evening a special meeting of the Indian Constituent Assembly was called. At midnight, to a background of wild celebrations in the streets, India became independent. The Indian political leaders had asked Lord Mountbatten to be the country's first Governor General. His first official duty was to swear in Nehru and his ministers as the first government of the new nation.

Nehru speaking to members of the Constituent Assembly at the midnight session: 'At the stroke of the midnight hour, when the world sleeps, India will awake to life and freedom. A moment comes which comes but rarely in history, when we step out from the old to the new, when an age ends and when the soul of a nation long suppressed finds utterance. It is fitting that at this solemn moment we take the pledge of dedication to the service of India and her people and to the still larger cause of humanity'.

The man who had done more than any other for the cause of Indian independence refused to attend the celebrations. Gandhi spent the day in Calcutta instead, praying and fasting. He was trying to put a stop to the communal violence there.

Communal violence

Villages of Muslim people which had celebrated Pakistan's Independence found themselves in India because the district around was largely Hindu. In the same way, Sikhs and Hindus found themselves in an isolated pocket of a Muslim state. Altogether, the Radcliffe Award left 5 million Sikhs and Hindus in Pakistan and 5 million Muslims in India. Few of them wanted to stay. They knew that their lands, their business, their religious buildings, their jobs would be seized by Hindus and Sikhs, or by Muslims. In a few days such seizures were taking place in every mixed area. In many cases the majority acted violently against the minority and violence with sticks and axes soon turned into vicious mob murders. As news of the first outrages spread so there were reprisals and mounting horrors with efforts to wipe out whole communities. It became unsafe to travel on a train unless it was guarded by soldiers of your community and even then there were ambushes and dreadful slaughters of women, children and men passengers.

Sabir Khan

In 1982 Sabir Khan was a teacher in a London school but in August 1947 he was living with his mother and grandfather in a house in the old part of Delhi. The family had come to Delhi in search of work from their home in east Punjab. Sabir's father was at the time fifty miles away in Punjab looking after the family land. Sabir was nine years old.

The family was Muslim as were many others who lived in that part of Delhi but apart from some festival times Sabir remembers little trouble between Hindus and Muslims. That all changed as Independence approached. Radio and newspapers began to carry stories of violence and murder. In Sabir's street, refugees began to appear from country areas outside Delhi, Muslims terrified of the Hindu mobs. People began to talk about going to Pakistan but at first Sabir's family didn't listen. After a while so many from their street had gone that Sabir's father, Khurshid, decided they should go too. It was not an easy decision because they would have to leave almost everything behind in India and start a new life in Pakistan. A place was found for Sabir on a special train leaving Delhi for Pakistan with Muslim civil servants. He went with an uncle, clutching a small metal trunk with the family jewellery and their best clothes. The train was guarded by soldiers and there were no attacks but Sabir was scared to death throughout the three days it took. There were lots of unexplained halts, one on a long bridge. Looking down into the valley below, Sabir saw many metal suitcases lying on the ground, broken open and looted.

The station at Lahore was in complete chaos when they got there. Many refugee trains had arrived but no arrangements had been made to deal with them. Sabir and his uncle spent three days on the platform. Someone stole Sabir's metal trunk while he was asleep. His uncle managed to get a place for them on a train to Karachi, the new capital, where they lived for ten months in rows of army tents called Jacob's Line. Meanwhile the rest of Sabir's family, after escaping from Delhi, his father disguised as a Hindu, had been unloaded from a refugee train at a place called Pirmahal. Here in Lyallpur District west of Lahore, the Khan family came together again. They were given a plot of reasonable farm land that had belonged to Hindus or Sikhs who had left their homes for the same reason as the Khans but in the opposite direction.

Sabir's family were, in some ways, quite fortunate. Hundreds of thousands lost their lives in these dreadful months but they were alive and able to make a new start in Pirmahal. Sabir went to school there, then on to Government College in Lyallpur, and then to study Law at the university in Lahore. His family made many claims for compensation from the Indian government for their lost property in what is now the Indian part of Punjab, and eventually received something.

The death of Gandhi

At five minutes past five on 30th January 1948, Gandhi left his simple room in Birla House, Delhi. He was late for his evening prayer meeting because he had been with Deputy Prime Minister Patel. Leaning as usual on his two young female relatives Abha and Manu, he made his way down the red sandstone path to the grass lawn where some 500 people waited. Less than a week before he had ended his fast in protest at the violence suffered by the Muslim population of Delhi. A handful of Hindu extremists felt that Gandhi was a traitor to the Hindu cause because he spoke up for Muslims. He even had parts of the Koran read out at his prayer meetings and encouraged Muslims to attend. Five days before, a young Hindu called Madan Lal had thrown a bomb at the evening meeting in an attempt to kill Gandhi but it missed and exploded harmlessly. Gandhi told the police not to harm Madan Lal. 'You should pity him,' he said.

As Gandhi climbed the five steps up to the prayer lawn, the crowd stood up and parted to let him get to the platform he sat on to lead the prayers. A young man pushed his way out of the crowd and stood before him as if to ask for his blessing. Manu took his hand to move him aside but he pushed her away so that she fell. He took a small automatic pistol from his pocket and from about two feet he shot Gandhi twice. 'Hey Rama' were Gandhi's last words as he staggered, one arm resting briefly on Abha's shoulder. A third shot, and Gandhi slumped to the ground. He died almost immediately.

The young man was called Nathuram Godse, a friend of Madan Lal. He was a newspaper editor from Poona, a Brahmin who hated Gandhi for his support of Muslims in Delhi. He was executed by hanging six months later.

Outside Birla House a huge crowd gathered, begging for a last sight of the body, so for a few hours it was placed tilted forward on the roof with a searchlight illuminating it. Millions marched with the funeral procession the following day and millions more watched. The body was cremated on the banks of the Jamuna River, Gandhi's third son Ramdas lighting the pyre. A few close personal friends received some ashes, some were sent to Burma, Tibet, Ceylon and Malaya but most were put into the rivers of India in huge ceremonies throughout the country.

Louis Fischer, his American friend and biographer, wrote this:

'On January 30th, 1948, the Friday he died, Mahatma Gandhi was what he had always been: a private citizen without wealth, property, official title, official post, academic distinction, scientific achievement, or artistic gift. Yet men with governments and armies behind them paid homage to the little man of seventy-eight in a loincloth.'

L. Fischer, *The Life of Mahatma Gandhi*, 1950.

Part of the procession of 'orphans' as many Indians regarded themselves after Gandhi's death. They accompanied the portion of Gandhi's ashes that were carried through Bombay to the sea. The ashes were scattered into the ocean and the people then bathed in the waters.

PART THREE

THE INDEPENDENT STATES

13
India 1947–71

India became the world's largest democracy at her Independence in 1947. The government which took power led by Jawaharlal Nehru was made up of leaders of Congress, the party which had won the elections in 1946 for a Constituent Assembly. The Constituent Assembly's tasks were to arrange for Independence and then agree on a constitution which would lay down the system of government and law for the new nation. Fourteen days after Independence the Assembly set up a Commission to begin this work. It took two years before the work was finished and the Constituent Assembly gave its agreement.

The Union of India

From January 1950 the country became the Union of India. There is an elected Assembly for each of the states which make up the Union and the leader of the largest party in the state becomes its Chief Minister. Laws for the Union are made in its own Houses of Parliament. The Rajya Sabha is the Council of States which has around 240 members chosen by the State Assemblies. However, the centre of political power is in the Lok Sabha (Lower House) which is similar in structure to the British House of Commons. Every adult Indian votes for one of the 540 or so members of the Lok Sabha and the government is chosen from the party which wins the largest number of seats. The President of India invites the leader of that party to form an administration.

The elections, 1952

The first General Election under the new constitution followed early in 1952. The Congress party swept to power throughout India and its leader Jawaharlal Nehru became the first Prime Minister. He was already established as a national leader and he quickly became a respected world statesman also. He remained Prime Minister until his death in 1964. With only a short break, Congress has ruled in India until recent times. Nehru's daughter and grandson were to follow him as Prime Minister.

Three Nehru generations. Nehru is pictured in 1950 with his daughter Indira Gandhi and his grandson Rajiv, both of whom followed him as premier of India.

The Planning Commission

Nehru believed that better standards of living for Indians would only come about by rapid growth in agriculture and industry throughout the country. Growth had to be rapid because the population was increasing so fast: in 1950 it was growing at 1.3 per cent each year; by 1960 the increase was 3 per cent or an extra 16 million people each year. At the time of independence, India had a population of around 350 million. By the mid-1980s, it had more than doubled to well over 700 million. One of the things Nehru had admired about the USSR was the way Stalin had used central planning to achieve rapid growth. In 1950 Nehru set up a Planning Commission for the whole of India. Its task was to make and carry out a plan to achieve these higher living standards. The Commission was given strong powers and massive funds.

Five Year Plans

The First Five Year Plan (1951–6) concentrated on increasing agricultural production. It was rather more successful than the Second Five Year Plan (1956–61) which concentrated on the development of large scale industry. The planners were aware that their experiment in democratic planning was probably the largest and most complex ever undertaken. They had, as Nehru said, 'a mighty theme'.

The Third Five Year Plan (1961–66) aimed to make India self-sufficient in basic foodstuffs and to increase the output of the country's own heavy industries, such as steel and chemicals, to cut down the amount of such products which had to be imported. Much of the money to carry out the scheme, some 8,000 million pounds, had to be borrowed from foreign countries, especially the USA.

Changes in society

Nehru believed that a vital part of the modernisation of India was to give respect to the rights of each individual. Gandhi had begun the attack on some traditional ways in India which denied such basic rights to millions of Indians. He had attacked the idea that some people – the so-called 'Untouchables' – could be considered so low in status as to be outside the social system altogether. He called them Harijans, the Children of God.

The 'Untouchables'

'Untouchability' was abolished in the 1950 Constitution of India, which gave the Harijans seventy reserved seats in the Lok Sabha. In 1955 the practice of treating people as 'Untouchables' was made an offence, punishable by prison. The Harijans were now, in theory, free to enter any place of worship, bathe in any stream, go to any shop as well as having equality in the law courts and as voters. The Five Year Plans set money aside to improve the position of Harijans by, for example, providing wells for them to use in villages where other villagers would not share water with them.

The laws and the special aid did not, however, abolish the social disadvantages suffered by Harijans. Few people were prosecuted for discriminating against them and they are often still barred from taking a full part in ordinary community life. However, the laws have encouraged groups of Harijans to band together to campaign against prejudice and discrimination.

Women

Nehru was also determined to improve the status of women in India. In 1955 the Hindu Succession Act was passed. This gave women equal rights with men in the inheritance and keeping of property. The following year came the Hindu Marriage Act. This gave a legal base for marriage to one partner (monogamy) and provided for support payment by a husband if he divorced his wife. Muslims in India continued to be governed by traditional Islamic law in questions relating to marriage.

Language

It had for some time been Congress policy that Hindi should replace

English as the language used in public affairs, the law courts, secondary education and so on. The 1950 Constitution laid down that this change should take place in 1965. However, Hindi is spoken by not many more than half the people of India. Many other groups have mother tongues which stem from Hindi but have gradually become different in the way they are spoken and written. In the south most people speak Dravidian languages such as Tamil and Telegu which are entirely different.

As Prime Minister, Nehru was faced with many demands that these other languages should be recognised as equal to Hindi. He agreed that some states could be officially bilingual so that Hindi and another language such as Punjabi or Gujerati were both recognised. In some cases this meant re-drawing the boundaries of states so that they matched the homelands of different language groups more closely. To meet the demands of the Dravidian language speakers he agreed that English could continue as an official language in the south for the foreseeable future. As almost all educated Hindi and Tamil speakers also use English, that meant that the people of the south would not suffer because they could not speak Hindi.

Kashmir

The one outstanding problem by the start of 1948 was that of the three Princely states, Hyderabad, Kashmir and Junagadh, which had not been persuaded by the Congress leaders and Mountbatten to join the Indian Union. There were also two small areas left over from the colonial past. France still governed Pondicherry, once their main trading base on the south-east Coromandel Coast. Portugal held on to the 100 kilometres of coast and nearly 4,000 square kilometres of Goa on the west coast below Bombay.

Junagadh and Hyderabad

The tiny seaport state of Junagadh on the coast of Gujerat and the huge southern state of Hyderabad did not have much in common. However, both had Muslim rulers over largely Hindu populations. The Nawab of Junagadh said that he wanted to join Pakistan. The Nizam of Hyderabad refused to join the Indian Union. In both cases the government sent in the Indian Army to take control. Both became part of India.

Kashmir

Kashmir was not so straightforward. This land of high mountain peaks and green valleys in the far north lies between India and Pakistan. In 1948 it had a Hindu ruler and a Hindu majority population in and around Jammu but in the Vale of Kashmir the population was mainly Muslim and in the mountains to the north and west Muslim hill chiefs were powerful.

With these complications it is not surprising that the Maharajah put off any decision about joining Pakistan or India. In October 1947 a force of Pathan tribesmen from the North-West Frontier attacked, aiming to capture Srinagar, the capital, to secure Kashmir for Pakistan.

The Maharajah immediately agreed to sign a treaty joining the Indian Union and appealed for support against the Pathan attack. Indian paratroops landed and saved Srinagar. Fighting broke out between the armies of Pakistan and India, lasting until early in 1949. Despite the ceasefire, Pakistan refused to accept India's actions in Kashmir. Tensions in the area became open warfare in 1965 and again in 1971. The Simla Agreement of 1973 established a ceasefire line which in effect partitioned Kashmir between India and Pakistan.

Pondicherry and Goa

As for the former colonies, the French agreed to accept India's claim to Pondicherry and handed it back in 1954. Portugal, however, still clung to her old colonial empire and refused to leave Goa. In 1961 the Indian army invaded Goa and it too became part of the Indian Union.

The Nagas

One small area did not want anything to do with either India or Pakistan in 1947. The Nagas, hill people in the far north-east of India on the border with Burma (see map, page vi), had been content with British administration which protected them from exploitation by the people living in the plains of Assam. Now they were to be governed by these same plains people. The Naga National Council led by Z. A. Phizo declared themselves independent in August 1947. This defiance by a mere half million hill people was ignored. The 1950 Indian constitution treated the Naga Hills as part of Assam Province.

In 1952 Phizo had a stormy meeting with Jawaharlal Nehru who refused to consider an independent Nagaland. By the start of 1955 armed police were drafted into the Naga Hills to deal with increasingly violent guerilla activity. The following year the whole area was declared 'disturbed' and put under the control of the Indian Army. In the two years that followed, official Naga deaths were put at 1,400 but there were persistent reports of atrocities by Indian Army troops in their anti-guerilla campaigns.

A ceasefire agreed in 1964 lasted for eight years, ended by the Indian government after an assassination attempt on the Chief Minister in the area. During that time the army had established posts in most villages and had built military roads. The guerillas had also lost their safe bases across the border in what had been East Pakistan.

The Naga guerillas fought on for another three years but in the end they had to accept military defeat. In November 1975 the Shillong Accord was signed. The Naga National Council accepted their status as Nagaland, a full, if small, state of the Indian Union. Three years earlier, the Indian government had completed a re-organisation of local boundaries in the north-east with the creation of three new states and one union territory, all based on the traditional homelands of local people and carved out of the state of Assam. The area has remained unsettled in recent years and unity has sometimes seemed a fragile thing in this wild and remote part of India.

Sikh separatism in Punjab

The greatest threat to the stability and unity of India since Independence has been the unrest in Punjab State. In 1947 Punjab was partitioned between India and Pakistan and saw its millions on the move in both directions across the new frontier. Most Sikhs moved east into India but as their leader Master Tara Singh said at the time, 'the Hindus got Hindustan, the Muslims got Pakistan. What did the Sikhs get?'

Indian Punjab quickly became the wealthiest state in the Indian Union. Sikhs dominated in the countryside but Punjabi Hindus controlled the cities. The enterprise of both groups, good irrigation and the 'green revolution' were behind the Punjab success story. Sikhs were only one third of the Punjabi population in 1951 but were prominent in business, politics and the army.

The Akali Dal – the Army of Immortals – the main Sikh political party, was not satisfied. As a small minority in India, with their own distinct religion and a proud history as a fiercely independent state, they wanted much more control in Punjab. Some even wanted an independent country for Sikhs, to be called Khalistan.

In 1955 the Akali Dal led mass demonstrations by Sikhs. The Indian government ordered the police to invade the Golden Temple in Amritsar, the most sacred temple for Sikhs and the rallying place for the Sikh agitation. Nehru stood firm and refused to give way to the Sikh leader's demands that the state should be divided so that there could be a smaller Punjab where Sikhs were in a clear majority. Ten years later in 1965 the new Sikh leader Sant Fateh Singh threatened to fast to death unless the government re-organised the area to give more power to Sikhs. This, and the outbreak of war with Pakistan, made the government agree. The area was split up into a new, mainly Hindu, state of Haryana and a smaller Punjab, where now just over half the population were Sikhs.

Even in this smaller Punjab, the Akali Dal did not gain political power. In the 1972 elections, Congress won in the state. Its new Chief Minister was Zail Singh, an ally of Mrs Indira Gandhi, the Prime Minister of India. Political defeat forced the Akali Dal leaders to restate their long-term aims in the hope that they could rebuild their support among Sikhs in Punjab and the rest of the country. In 1973 they met at the city of Anandpur Sahib and wrote a new political programme. This 'Anandpur Sahib Resolution' claimed that the 'Akali Dal is the very embodiment of the hopes and aspirations of the Sikh nation'. It demanded that all the main centres of Sikh population should be merged with Punjab to create a single 'unit where the interests of Sikhs and Sikhism are specifically protected'. This new state, they urged, should have equal representation with all other states in the Union.

In 1977 the Akali Dal did achieve power in Punjab by allying with Janata, the party which had won the elections which turned Mrs Gandhi and Congress from power. By 1979, however, the new Indian

The Golden Temple of Amritsar, the most sacred temple of the Sikhs and the centre of Sikh unrest in Punjab. This photograph was taken in 1968, but the temple was damaged in fighting in 1984. However it has since been restored in every detail, precisely as before.

government was breaking into quarrelling groups and so was the Akali Dal. Many of its more extreme members broke away to join the militant movement of Jarnail Singh Bhindranwale. In the 1980s Bhindranwale was to pose a much more serious threat to the peace of Punjab and to the unity of India (see page 97).

War with China

On India's far north-eastern frontier there had long been territory claimed by both China and India. By 1960 China decided to use her military power to take back territory along the frontier south of Tibet which was now again under Chinese control. Tension rose, especially in the border area which India then called the North-East Frontier Region. Indian troops moved to the area in October 1962. There were clashes with Chinese troops and in November that year the Indian troops suffered a humiliating defeat and were driven back.

Nehru had always argued that the Asian states could solve their differences by negotiation rather than fighting. For many years he had kept friendly relations with communist China when she was isolated from the rest of the world. Now that policy was criticised as being responsible for India's defeat in the frontier war. His reputation in foreign affairs dimmed just as his efforts to expand industry and agriculture were failing to keep pace with the rise in population.

After Nehru

Two years after the frontier war with China, Nehru died. The men who chose his successor as Prime Minister were the powerful leaders of Congress Party groups throughout the country. They selected Lal Bahadur Shastri, a dedicated and experienced party worker with a reputation as a conciliator. Other people who were better known politically were ignored.

Shastri was faced with many difficult issues. In January 1965 Hindi was proclaimed the only national language despite Nehru's assurance. There were serious riots in the south. Congress then passed a law saying that English and Hindi should both be official languages. Then in March 1965 border incidents with Pakistan increased and by the summer these led to full-scale war. The Indian army halted Pakistan's attack and counter-attacked towards Lahore.

The USSR acted as a mediator between India and Pakistan, arranging a Peace Conference at Tashkent in Soviet Central Asia in January 1966. Both sides agreed to return to their pre-war positions. Public criticism of Shastri for this was halted by his sudden death in Tashkent at the end of the Peace Conference. He had been Prime Minister for eighteen months.

Indira Gandhi

Once again the Congress Party's inner group of leaders met to decide on a new Prime Minister. This time there was public argument as some leading Congress members were in favour of Morarji Desai. But he was disliked by others for his policies of encouraging close relations with the USA and opposing state control of parts of industry and agriculture. To stop Desai taking power, opponents agreed on Nehru's daughter, Indira Gandhi. It may be that they hoped she would be inexperienced enough to let them exercise real power in India. She had kept house for her father after his wife died but had not been active politically in his lifetime. Her marriage to Feroze Gandhi, a Parsi journalist and no relation to Mohandas Gandhi, had not lasted. After Nehru's death, she had become Minister of Information in Shastri's cabinet.

The Congress Party in Parliament voted on the two candidates. Morarji Desai won 169 votes against Indira Gandhi's 355. One reason for her victory was that Congress wanted an acceptable figurehead to lead the Party in the elections of 1967. In fact Congress kept its majority in the central Parliament but only by forty seats. It lost control of eight of the sixteen states. In Madras a Dravidian party, the DMK, came to power. In the state of Kerala the Communist Party of India ruled. The all-India supremacy of the Congress Party was shattered.

Indira Gandhi began to manage this difficult political situation with unexpected skill. Congress soon began to realise that she would not be a mere token leader. She appointed Desai as Deputy Prime Minister and set about establishing herself in India and abroad.

The showdown with the Congress Party leaders came in 1969. In the summer President Hussain died and the people who ran the Congress organisation wanted to appoint Sanjiva Reddy, a conservative. Indira Gandhi wanted the more radical Vice President V. V. Giri to be appointed. She saw this as the chance to establish that she was not under the thumb of the Congress leaders.

She sacked Morarji Desai as Finance Minister and forced him to resign as Deputy Prime Minister. Three days later she nationalised the leading banks. This was popular with many people in the country and meant that she could stand up to the Congress leaders. The result was a party split: 310 Congress MPs voted to back her and 119 voted for her removal as Prime Minister. There were now two Congress Parties. The one led by Indira Gandhi was known as Congress(Indira) or Congress(I).

14
Pakistan 1947–71

By 1947 the Muslim peoples in the north-west of British India and in East Bengal had come to believe in the idea of Pakistan rather than take their chances as a religious minority in an undivided, independent India. Many millions of Muslims did, in fact, stay in India. Many more left to make a new start in Pakistan. Out of the chaos and suffering came a fierce determination to make it work.

The laws and customs of Islam affect almost every aspect of society and politics in Pakistan. Islam gives Pakistan a national purpose and identity. This is a powerful force for unity but it was not enough on its own to prevent the break-up of the country in 1971.

A divided state   Jinnah talked of the Pakistan created by Partition as 'moth-eaten'. East and West Pakistan, separated by over 1,000 miles of India, had little in common except their religion. The economy of the new state was always going to be a cause of disputes. Partition had created some particular problems. For example, Pakistan produced cotton but it had always been milled in cities that remained in India. East Pakistan was the world's largest producer of jute but the jute mills were in and around Calcutta, now in India. Of the major ports, only Karachi went to Pakistan.

The new state lacked the basis for effective central government in its early days, without personnel, equipment or a capital city. Above all it had to cope with the millions of refugees of the Partition period.

The outbreak of the Korean War in 1950 was good news for the economy of Pakistan. World prices of jute, cotton and wool rose sharply because Korea had produced these things. New jute and cotton mills were built in Pakistan to satisfy this surge in demand.

After Jinnah

At Independence Jinnah's authority was supreme. As President of the Assembly as well as its legal adviser, he was the ruler of Pakistan. He

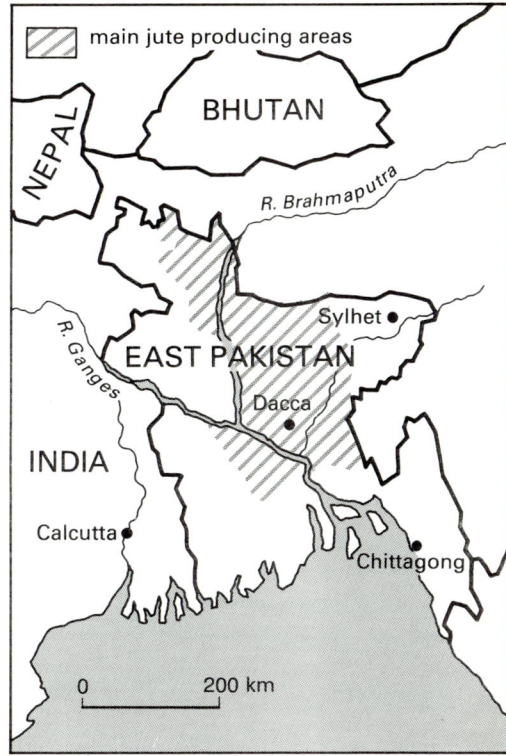

Pakistan in 1947.

was most concerned about three things – law and order, bribery and corruption, and equal rights for all citizens of Pakistan. At the first meeting of the Constituent Assembly on 11th August, 1947 he declared:

> 'You are free; you are free to go to your temples, you are free to go to your mosques or to any other place of worship in this State of Pakistan. You may belong to any religion or caste or creed – that has nothing to do with the business of the State... We are starting in the days when there is no discrimination, no distinction between one community and another, no discrimination between one caste or creed and another.'

Jinnah's death in September 1948 cut short these campaigns to end corruption and discrimination and Pakistan plunged into a political crisis.

Liaquat Ali Khan His natural successor was Liaquat Ali Khan, a long-standing colleague of Jinnah's from the struggle for independence. He was known as the Quaid-i-Millet, the Leader of the Community, but even so he lacked Jinnah's authority. The Muslim League had grown during the struggle for independence from British rule. As a political organisation it was much less effective at developing plans to cope with independent Pakistan's economic and social difficulties. The League also suffered because it could not satisfy the high hopes that had been raised during the Independence campaign.

The Assembly was itself divided. Powerful groups of members spoke for the individual provinces, for the refugees, even for the Hindu minority in East Pakistan. Few spoke for Pakistan as a whole. Even more serious for the new nation was the growing feeling in the senior ranks of the army of Pakistan that the country should take a more aggressive attitude towards India over Kashmir. In March 1951 the army chief and several other senior officers were arrested for planning a military take-over of the government. This came to be called the Rawalpindi Conspiracy. The officers were tried and put in prison but general discontent in the country did not go away.

Liaquat Ali Khan was assassinated a few months later in Rawalpindi. It is not clear exactly who killed him but his death meant that Pakistan had lost its two most able and experienced leaders in the first four years of its life. The new Governor General, Ghulam Mohammad, used his power base in Punjab to bid for leadership. In 1953 he imposed martial law on Punjab and direct rule over East Pakistan.

Powerful groups in Pakistan

Political leaders in Pakistan were able to stay in power because they had the support of the army and the officials of the civil service. It was these two groups, mostly trained by the British in undivided India, who had kept the government of Pakistan working during the difficult early years of the new nation. Very few senior officials or senior army officers were Bengalis, a situation much resented in East Pakistan.

The fact that Ghulam Mohammad and other leaders had to rely so much on the army and on the officials tended to undermine the authority of elected politicians in Pakistan. This was especially the case in East Pakistan and in the Province of Sind in West Pakistan. In Punjab and the North-West Frontier Province (NWFP), leading families were well represented in both politics and in government or army service.

Many politicians came from the great landowning families of Pakistan and often put the interests of their family or province before the interests of the State as a whole. Other provinces feared that Punjab wanted to dominate Pakistan. Many in West Pakistan worried that East Pakistan, which had a larger population, would have more influence if every adult were given the right to vote.

In many local areas, especially the countryside, ordinary people thought it their duty to vote for and to support their local landowner, whatever his policies or personality. Even so, the group with the greatest popular influence in Pakistan were the *ulema*.

The *ulema* There are no priests in Islam but religious leaders, teachers and guardians of Muslim law and tradition, are the *ulema*. They believe that Islam is the basis of society within Pakistan and look for support for this view from their political leaders. Liaquat Ali Khan described the State of Pakistan as a sacred trust from God and declared that it was a nation where 'the principles of democracy, freedom, equality, tolerance and social justice, as enunciated by Islam, shall be fully observed'.

The traditional *ulema* felt that the government should let them guide and unite the people of Pakistan by interpreting the traditional law. Many politicians, often lawyers themselves, preferred to use the system of courts and justice based on the British tradition.

Support of the USA

In the 1950s and especially after the end of the Korean War in 1953, the United States was determined to build up those countries in the world that could act as a buffer to the spread of communism. Pakistan, with its borders with China and Afghanistan, was just such a country.

In 1954 Pakistan signed the Mutual Defence Agreement with the USA. This meant that the United States would give massive aid to build up the armed forces of Pakistan and loans to make her economy stronger. Pakistan also became a member of the South-East Asia Treaty Organisation (SEATO), a military alliance of many non-communist countries with interests in South-East Asia which included Britain and France as well as the USA.

In 1955 Pakistan signed the Baghdad Pact, joining in a military alliance with Britain, Turkey, Iran and Iraq. When Iraq left this group in 1959 the alliance became CENTO, the Central Treaty Organisation.

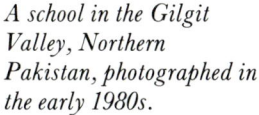

A school in the Gilgit Valley, Northern Pakistan, photographed in the early 1980s.

Pressure on the government to join the alliances and accept military aid on a large scale from the USA had come from army leaders. With the economy of Pakistan heading for thin times again with the end of the Korean War, it was their only chance of getting the new equipment they felt they needed to keep on terms with the much larger Indian army.

The collapse of the parliamentary system 1956–58

The Muslim League had been the most powerful political party in the government of Pakistan's provinces in the early years after Independence. However, it began to break up as new political parties arose, mainly with a strong base in one province. The elections for provincial governments in 1954 showed how far this break-up of the Muslim League had gone. It lost all power in East Pakistan to a coalition of the Awami (People's) League and the Krishak Sramik Party (Peasants and Workers Party). It also lost a lot of seats in the Assembly to parties representing the interests of provinces of West Pakistan.

Hussain Shaheed Suhrawardy, leader of the Awami League, became Prime Minister of Pakistan in 1956 but soon found that the hostility of many politicians in West Pakistan made his position difficult. In 1957 President Iskander Mirza sacked him. The political crisis soon became violent. In the Assembly in Dacca, East Pakistan, there was fighting in which members were killed. The Chief Minister of West Pakistan was assassinated. Provincial leaders in NWFP and Baluchistan declared that they wanted to break away from Pakistan.

These conflicts between the different provinces of Pakistan led to the first attempt to give it a system of government through a constitution. This laid down that the provinces of West Pakistan would be abolished and elections held for an Assembly with equal numbers coming from West and East Pakistan. By then, however, army leaders had lost patience with the politicians.

In October 1958 President Iskander Mirza, a former soldier, declared martial law, suspended the constitution and cancelled the elections due for early 1959. He had the full support of the army and government officials. In less than three weeks Mirza had fallen from power. He had made the mistake of trying to move against the commander-in-chief of the army, General Ayub Khan. The General had Mirza arrested and put on a plane for London.

The rule of General Ayub Khan

General Ayub had been known as a good administrator and a mediator. He had taken no part in politics until 1958 and as a member of a small tribe from NWFP he had no debts to any of the major groups in Pakistan. He soon became a powerful political figure.

Opposition political leaders were intimidated, various newspapers were closed down and others taken under government control. Army courts were set up to try many cases of corruption. The *ulema* were warned not to allow political discussion in mosques.

By early 1959 General Ayub felt confident enough to send the army back to their barracks. On the whole government officials were allowed to run the country.

Some steps were taken to ease tension in East Pakistan. Government investment in East Pakistan was to be increased rapidly and Dacca was to become another national capital. Important government bodies like the Planning Commission were told to hold meetings in Dacca.

In 1958 General Ayub set up a Land Reform Commission. It tried to tackle the problem of the huge amounts of land owned by a few families. Acting on its advice the government put limits on the amount of land that could be owned by any individual. They claimed to have broken the power of the great landholders but in practice little changed. There were usually ways around the new laws.

In 1960 the World Bank arranged huge loans to supply aid and technical assistance to Pakistan. Money and advisers poured into Pakistan. With this sort of support and a period of political stability, the 1960s were years of rapid economic growth – but the spread of wealth was uneven. East Pakistan gained little benefit. A huge proportion of the wealth of the country was still in the hands of a few great landowning and trading families in West Pakistan said to number twenty-three.

The 1962 Constitution

In 1962 General Ayub announced a new constitution for the country. It gave the President considerable power but relaxed some aspects of military rule. Late in the year, the ban on political parties was lifted. The Muslim League, declared by General Ayub as the official government party, now had opposition.

These opposition parties combined to fight General Ayub in the elections for President held in 1965. They chose Jinnah's sister Fatima as their candidate. General Ayub won comfortably in West Pakistan but narrowly in East Pakistan. The election had shown the growing strength of opposition to his rule.

War with India, 1965

War with India in 1965 over Kashmir and other border disputes came to an end in September that year. Britain and the USA had cut off military and other supplies to both sides to get them to stop fighting. Pakistan, with its heavy reliance on the USA, was especially badly hit. Lives had been lost. Pride had been dented. There was nothing to show for it and public opinion in Pakistan was hostile. There were demonstrations in Lahore and Karachi against the USA. When President Ayub signed the peace agreement with Prime Minister Shastri of India in Tashkent early in 1966, reaction at home was angry.

Opposition mounted. Sheikh Mujibur Rahman, the leader of the Awami League in East Pakistan, was demanding much greater self-government for Bengal. President Ayub's Foreign Minister, Zulfikar Ali Bhutto, resigned from the government and founded a new party, the Pakistan People's Party (PPP). Ayub's serious illness early in 1968 further weakened his power.

Mob violence spread. The army moved into major cities but found it difficult to regain control. In East Pakistan things were even worse. In March 1969 martial law was again declared. At that point Ayub Khan, a sick man, handed over to another general, Yahya Khan.

Zulfikar Ali Bhutto   At the end of 1969 Yahya Khan announced that the military government would give way to civilian rule by the end of the following year. Throughout 1970 the various political parties campaigned for support. The strongest party in West Pakistan was the PPP led by Zulfikar Ali Bhutto. Under their slogan 'Islam Our Faith, Democracy Our Policy, and Socialism our Economy' their campaign appealed to the people of the villages and the poorer districts of towns. It promised *roti, kapra aur makan* – bread, clothes and housing. In East Pakistan Sheikh Mujibur Rahman led the Awami League which gained widespread support for their six-point policy of semi-independence from West Pakistan.

The elections were held at last in December 1970. The PPP won a large majority in West Pakistan with particularly strong support in Punjab and Sind. The victory of the Awami League in East Pakistan was even more decisive. They won 167 out of a possible 169 seats.

Any settlement for Pakistan as a whole depended on an agreement between Sheikh Mujibur for East Pakistan, Bhutto for West Pakistan and Yahya Khan for the ruling military government. These talks began in the early months of 1971.

15

The birth of Bangladesh

The Awami League

The elections in Pakistan held at the end of 1970 left General Yahya Khan, the military ruler, with a most difficult situation. He had announced a return to civilian rule in Pakistan and had called the elections. The Awami League had won almost every seat in East Pakistan and their leader Sheikh Mujibur Rahman claimed that he should form an Awami League government to rule the whole of Pakistan. This was because a majority of Pakistan's huge population lived in the East. Zulfikar Ali Bhutto, leader of the PPP who had won a large majority in West Pakistan, refused to accept the right of Sheikh Mujib and the Awami League to form a government and to draw up a new constitution for the whole of Pakistan. Bhutto was especially unwilling to accept the Awami League because they insisted on their six-point programme. This would give East Pakistan a considerable degree of independence within Pakistan.

The quarrel between East and West Pakistan

At the heart of the quarrel between Mujib and Bhutto was the tension built into the creation of Pakistan in 1947. The West and East had little in common except their religion. Neither part would accept, for long, rule by the other. In the East they felt that they had been dominated by the West ever since 1947. Top jobs in the army and civil service went to those from West Pakistan.

The economic inequality was even more important. East Pakistan's most important product was jute which can be made into ropes and sacking. Nearly all of it went to West Pakistan where it was processed by workers there and sold overseas by West Pakistani traders. In 1959 the income per head in East Pakistan was only three-quarters what it was in West Pakistan. By 1970 it had fallen to two-thirds of the West Pakistani level. East Pakistan had more than half the population but got less than half of government spending on public services and schemes to develop industry and agriculture.

Unable to get Mujib and Bhutto to agree, Yahya Khan lost patience. In March 1971 he re-imposed military Government in Pakistan and refused to allow the newly-elected Parliament to meet. Reaction in East Pakistan was violent. There were strikes, marches and demonstrations. Sheikh Mujib told his people to stop paying taxes, to ignore new censorship laws and to halt public services like transport. It was a direct challenge to Yahya Khan.

Sheikh Mujib announces the birth of Bangladesh

Yahya Khan and Bhutto flew to Dacca in a last attempt to reach agreement. Mujib would have none of it. General Tikka Khan, military Governor in East Pakistan, put long prepared plans into operation. The army took over in Dacca and other main cities in the East. Road-blocks and barriers appeared. Mujib just had time to announce the birth of the 'sovereign independent People's Republic of Bangladesh' before he was arrested at his home in Dacca and sent under heavy guard to prison in West Pakistan.

Other Awami League leaders managed to escape the arrests and in a town called Mujibnagar near the Indian border they proclaimed the Independence of Bangladesh on 17th April 1971. Mujib was named as President.

Resistance

Very soon fierce fighting broke out in Dacca and other major cities of East Pakistan. The Bangladeshi resistance fighters formed a Liberation Army, the Mukti Bahini, commanded by a retired army officer, Colonel Osmany. Most of his fighters were volunteers, farmers, students and professional people who shared a determination to fight for the survival of the new-born Bangladesh. Many paid the price with their lives. Pakistan army units with Bengali soldiers deserted and crossed over with their arms and equipment to join the Mukti Bahini. The most highly trained of these troops were the East Bengal Regiment but they were joined by a paramilitary force, the East Pakistan Rifles, and units of the East Pakistan police.

The Mukti Bahini Even with these recruits and their equipment, Colonel Osmany and the Mukti Bahini seemed to have little chance of victory. The Pakistani commander, General Tikka Khan, had 60,000 regular troops, mostly from West Pakistan, with heavy guns and armoured vehicles. The Mukti Bahini was able to move freely only near the Indian border and most of its forces crossed into India to set up training camps. Along with them went a stream of refugees fleeing to avoid massacre. More than a quarter of a million crossed into India in the first few days and in six months the number had grown to nearly 10 million.

India's relations with Pakistan had been bad for many years, especially since the fighting over Kashmir. She also wished to see the return of the millions of refugees who were crowded into some of the poorest parts of India. The Indian government gave the Mukti Bahini a great deal of help with training and supplies of military equipment. In July, Colonel Osmany felt strong enough to leave the Indian camps and launch the Monsoon Offensive, hoping to take advantage of the wet conditions.

The Monsoon Offensive was held and driven back by the Pakistan army. The government felt so confident that Tikka Khan was allowed to return to West Pakistan to be replaced as army commander in the East by General Niazi. However, the Mukti Bahini had performed well enough to lead the government of Pakistan to increase its forces in the East to 80,000.

India invades East Pakistan

Full-scale war between India and Pakistan had been brewing for months. Tension in border areas in both East and West had increased, with occasional shelling. In late November 1971 Pakistan accused India of sending troops across the border into East Pakistan. In response early in December the Pakistan air force attacked military targets in northern India including air bases. The following day, 4th December, India launched a full-scale land, sea and air invasion of East Pakistan. At the same time the Indian air force quickly gained air superiority and attacked targets in West Pakistan.

The Indian government had planned their invasion of East Pakistan well in advance. When they invaded, the Pakistan army was dispersed on border duties and anti-rebel operations and in no shape to hold a coordinated attack by regular troops in much larger numbers.

India's nine infantry divisions, supported by three Mukti Bahini brigades, struck hard and fast at Dacca, the capital, by-passing other cities. The Pakistan army fought desperately but without supplies and no means of retreat they had little chance. Dacca fell to the Indian army and the Mukti Bahini on 16th December 1971. General Niazi surrendered with about 75,000 men to General Aurora, the Indian commander. India declared a ceasefire on its western front the same day and Pakistan did the same the day after.

The fall of Yahya Khan

In West Pakistan these events were followed by days of increasingly savage rioting against the now widely unpopular government of General Yahya Khan. Faced with a rapidly deteriorating situation, Yahya Khan had no choice. He resigned on 20th December to be replaced as President by Zulfikar Ali Bhutto.

Residents of Dacca search their bombed homes for survivors during the India–Pakistan war.

One of Bhutto's first actions was to release Sheikh Mujib from prison. Talks between the two leaders in Rawalpindi did little to bridge the gap between them but the public mood in West Pakistan was clearly in favour of Mujib's return to Bangladesh. Sheikh Mujib returned in triumph to Dacca on 11th January, 1972 to receive a hero's welcome from the people of Bangladesh. He started work as Prime Minister the following day, leading a government of his Awami League party.

A new republic

At the end of the year a constitution stated that Bangladesh was to be a republic, with free elections, a democratic Parliament and tolerance in religion. However, harsh realities soon made themselves felt. An estimated 250,000 women and girls were officially described as 'war-affected' during the civil war. These rape victims were considered socially unfit for marriage and had little future in a traditional society.

Many were cast out by their families. Government efforts to help those victims met with little success. Estimates of the uncounted war dead vary from 1 to 3 million. 10 million had fled as refugees to India. Thousands of schools were destroyed and many teachers killed. The transport system was all but destroyed. Starvation, always just around the corner even in this fertile land, edged closer.

Before 1971 most important officials and businessmen had been from West Pakistan. This had been one major grievance of Bengalis. These officials fled to Pakistan or were killed, leaving the new government to face its problems with inexperienced, untried officials. Nearly half a million heavily armed guerilla fighters, the Mukti Bahini and others, had to be disarmed and taught the arts of peace. Most did return to their old lives but many turned to violent crime.

One of the first acts of the new government was to nationalise major industries, all transport and many banks. At the same time legal protection from prosecution was withdrawn from civil servants, a clear sign that Mujib did not wish the country to be run either by civilian or by military officials. In their place the role of the Awami League grew. In the middle of 1972 a paramilitary village security force was created by the Awami League to bring law and order to rural areas. Called the Rakkhi Bahini, the Defence Force, its first recruits were former guerilla fighters.

By 1975 the Rakkhi Bahini was 30,000 strong, with plans to grow to five times that number. It was well armed and paid and was not under the control of either army or police but answered directly to Sheikh Mujib. Opponents began to talk openly of 'Mujib's private army'. If the Rakkhi Bahini was supposed to protect villagers from crime and violence, they said, who was to protect the villagers from the Rakkhi Bahini?

Even so Sheikh Mujib was wildly popular in his first years as Prime Minister of Bangladesh. His Awami League won nearly 98 per cent of the vote in the 1973 elections. Mujib was revered as 'Banga-bandhu', the Friend of Bengal. He more than any other was seen as responsible for the birth of the new nation. The new national anthem summed up the mood:

'Amar Sonar Bangla, ami tomay bhalobashi.'
'My golden Bengal, I love you.'

16
Into the 1980s

India

Mrs Indira Gandhi became Prime Minister of India in 1966. Three years later she made a decisive break with the Congress Party leaders who had appointed her. Now undisputed leader of her Congress (Indira) party she set about tackling the enormous tasks she had inherited.

Jawaharlal Nehru, her father, had concentrated on his important

Indira Gandhi photographed in the garden of her home in 1968, shortly after she became Prime Minister.

role as world statesman in the later years of his life. Tensions within Indian society and politics had grown. Nehru's death had left a huge gap in Indian public life. He had led India to Independence and was not easily replaced. Congress leaders had thought that his daughter Indira would act as a suitable figurehead for their own control of the nation.

Indira Gandhi had had other ideas. Her bold and determined capture of power in the Congress Party in 1969 made many powerful enemies amongst the senior Congress men she had thrown aside (see page 83). She had little time for people she thought had less energy and vision than she had.

Emergency, 1975

Charges were brought against Mrs Gandhi by her opponents, accusing her of corruption in an election. In 1975 she was tried on these charges and found guilty of using civil servants to work for her election campaign. In reply she accused her political enemies of trying to overthrow her government and democracy itself. She made an Emergency Declaration, giving her government very wide powers. Opposition politicians were arrested, newspapers were censored. Her ambitious younger son Sanjay, a leader of the Congress Youth Movement, became an important influence on his mother during the two years of the Emergency which lasted from 1975 to 1977. In particular Sanjay was later accused of pushing the population control campaign so hard that harsh and unacceptable methods were used by local Congress officials. These stories caused outrage in India and overseas. In March 1977 Mrs Gandhi ended the Emergency and called an election. She was heavily defeated and Congress was swept from power.

During the next few years the government formed by the various opposition parties proved ineffective. Government ministers used their energies to fight each other. In the elections of January 1980 Mrs Gandhi and Congress (I) won a huge victory and she was returned to power in triumph. Triumph was followed by tragedy. In June 1980 her son Sanjay was killed when his light plane crashed.

Sikh unrest

There were other acute problems to be faced that year. In Punjab a new and fiercer sort of Sikh action developed, led by a little known village preacher called Jarnail Singh Bhindranwale. Arrested in 1981 for the second of two murders, Bhindranwale's fierce support, especially among younger Sikhs from poorer farming areas, forced his release from prison. In 1982 he moved into the Golden Temple in Amritsar, the centre of the Sikh religion. There, surrounded by guards armed with swords and rifles, he organised gangs of Sikh youths as they carried out attacks and murders in the Punjab countryside.

Throughout 1983 these motorcycle hit squads got bolder. Many of the victims were Hindus, and innocent Sikhs were attacked in revenge. Faced with this crisis, the government set aside the authority of Punjab State and declared President's Rule. The killings continued.

By the middle of 1984 the Indian government decided that direct military action was the only way to deal with Bhindranwale and his followers. Indira Gandhi ordered the army to attack and capture the Golden Temple at all costs. Code named 'Operation Bluestar', the attack was launched on 1st June 1984. Only after five days of bitter fighting was it all over. The defenders fought to the death, perhaps 1,000 in all. The army, which had to bring in tanks to end it, lost some 200 troops. Many of the most holy buildings of the Golden Temple were severely damaged.

Murder of Mrs Gandhi

Jarnail Singh Bhindranwale died with most of his followers but a few escaped just before the army attacked. They wanted revenge. Other Sikhs, shocked by the attack on their holiest temple, could never forgive Indira Gandhi for ordering the army in. Her security advisers told her that Sikhs should be kept well away but she refused to listen. She took pride in showing foreign visitors that she still had Sikhs among her closest security guards. On 31st October, 1984, as she walked through the garden of her house at 1 Safdarjang Road, New Delhi, she was murdered by two of her Sikh bodyguards.

The day before she was killed she had said, 'Every drop of my blood, I'm sure, will contribute to the growth of the nation.' For several days much more blood was shed in Delhi. Hindu mobs attacked and murdered any Sikhs they could find. Rajiv Gandhi, as the eldest son, lit his mother Indira's funeral pyre of sandalwood. A few days later he was appointed Prime Minister of a badly shaken India by the ruling Congress Party until elections could be held. Congress(I) won a huge majority in the December 1984 elections. Rajiv Gandhi was swept to power as Prime Minister on a wave of emotion at the murder of his mother.

The Indian Nation

Despite Nagaland and Punjab, despite the wish of different language groups to protect their identity, the unity of India has never been seriously at risk. The social system, still partly based on caste, is often deeply unfair. In modern India it is illegal to discriminate against someone because of their caste group, but it happens all the time, especially in the rural areas. It does provide, however, a well understood framework. The civil service is another important part of the national structure. It is often slow and sometimes corrupt but it has avoided being drawn too obviously into serving the political parties rather than the people of India. The army has not seen the need to replace the politicians with its rule, as has happened in many of India's neighbours in Asia. Three wars with Pakistan since 1947 have left many Indians expecting another war before too long. Throughout the 1970s and 1980s there were persistent stories in India that Pakistan was giving shelter and training to Sikh terrorists. Whether or not these fears about Pakistan were real or imaginary, they help give Indians a sense of belonging to a nation which will survive if its people are loyal to its form of government.

India is a major Asian power and acts accordingly. In 1982 the Asian Games were held in Delhi. Organising this event and the major construction programme that went with it was the first major public task undertaken by Rajiv Gandhi for the then Prime Minister, his mother. Indians with an interest in politics support such events, which underline the importance of India as one of the Non-aligned nations which try to act independently of the great power groups dominated by the USSR and USA.

The 1989 elections

In the November 1989 elections, Congress(I) lost power to the National Front, a loose group of opposition parties led by V. P. Singh who became the new Prime Minister. Congress(I) remained the largest single party, led now in opposition by Rajiv Gandhi.

In November 1990 Singh was himself replaced as Prime Minister by Chandra Shekhar, a rival National Front Leader.

Pakistan

President Bhutto

In December 1970 Zulfikar Ali Bhutto became President of Pakistan. He had political control of a country reeling from the breakaway of its entire Eastern Province, the new nation of Bangladesh (see page 92). The army of Pakistan had suffered a major setback, defeated in Bengal by the Indian army and the Mukti Bahini. They had also come off worst in fighting on India's western front.

The humiliation of the loss of East Pakistan caused the fall from power of the previous President, General Yahya Khan. Bhutto inherited an unsettled country. Rivalries still existed between Pakistan's four remaining provinces – Punjab, Sind, Baluchistan and NWFP.

When Britain officially recognised the new nation of Bangladesh by sending an ambassador to Dacca in 1972, President Bhutto decided that Pakistan must leave the Commonwealth in protest. Instead, he worked for much closer ties with other Islamic countries.

Bhutto and his Pakistan People's Party had campaigned on a radical programme which claimed it would give top priority to the needs and rights of ordinary citizens. In power he tried to carry out radical measures which included nationalising many industries as well as banking and insurance companies. Laws were passed to transfer some land from the richest landowners to peasant farmers. Bhutto himself came from a wealthy landowning family in Sind Province. His political support came mainly from Sind and Punjab, where the great majority of Pakistanis live. PPP was not popular in the other two provinces. It won only 15 per cent of the vote in NWFP in the 1970 elections and only 2 per cent in Baluchistan. The governments of Baluchistan and NWFP resisted many of Bhutto's new laws and he drove them from power. Between 1973 and 1977 there was a rebellion in Baluchistan against the central government. Some 5,000 people were killed. Crops and livestock were destroyed. Around 3,000 regular troops were killed but some *sardars*, tribal chiefs, continued to resist.

General Zia

By 1977 most political organisations in the country had lined up against the PPP and in April the leading unions called for a general strike. Bhutto's reply was to order martial law in the main towns. The responsibility for carrying out these orders was given to the Chief of Staff, General Zia-ul-Haq. On the night of 4th July, General Zia ordered the army to arrest President Bhutto and all the main PPP leaders, and on the next day the army took over the government.

Two years later Mr Bhutto was put on trial accused of arranging the murder of a political opponent, found guilty and hanged. General Zia put the brakes on many of Bhutto's plans, including the concentration of power at the centre. The military government led by General Zia had the support of powerful groups in Pakistan – business interests, landowners, and the *ulema*, the religious leaders of Islam. The General set up a Council of Islamic Ideology to make sure that the principles of Islam remained an important part of the life of the nation.

Early in 1985 elections were held and eight years of martial law came to an end. Early in 1986 Mohammad Khan Junejo, leader of the Muslim League, became Prime Minister. General Zia remained President and political activities were still firmly limited. Mr Bhutto's old party, the Pakistan People's Party, was the largest opposition group but a divided one. The return to Pakistan in 1986 of Mr Bhutto's daughter Benazir, campaigning against General Zia, drew large crowds and popular support, especially in Sind.

General Zia-ul-Haq at the annual 'Pakistan Day Parade' at Rawalpindi in 1979.

Late in 1986 communal violence between Pathans and Bihari immigrants from Bangladesh in Karachi, Pakistan's largest city, lasted for days and left many dead. In the North-West Frontier Province, homeland of the Pathans, the estimated 3 million refugees from across the border in Afghanistan were a major problem for the government. Arms and drug smuggling across the border into Pakistan became an even greater problem than usual in the area. Often the arms and drugs were brought down to Karachi, Pakistan's only major port. It was a large police operation in Karachi which was said to have sparked off the communal violence of 1986. The Pathan drugs gangs blamed the Biharis for helping the police.

In the middle of August 1988, the military transport plane carrying President Zia exploded in mid-air near the desert city of Bahawalpur. Zia was killed, as were five army generals and the US ambassador.

Benazir Bhutto

In the months that followed it was clear that Pakistan's political leaders were ready to seize this chance to dismantle military rule and replace it with party politics. Elections were announced for December but until they had taken place no one was sure whether the army would give up its control of the country. When the votes were counted they showed that the PPP had won by far the largest number of seats in Parliament. Benazir Bhutto became Prime Minister, the first woman to take power in a Muslim country. The leading opposition group was the Islamic Democratic Alliance (IDA) headed by Nawaz Sharif. He became Chief Minister of Punjab Province so that Benazir Bhutto's government was faced with a problem which was similar to her father's: a large part of Pakistan's population had a provincial government which was opposed to the national government in Islamabad.

After just twenty months in power, Benazir Bhutto was dismissed by President Khan in August 1990. She was replaced as Prime Minister by Ghulam Mustafa Jatoi who, with IDA support, went on to defeat Bhutto and the PPP in the October 1990 election.

Bangladesh

In the first months of independence Sheikh Mujib's policies were clearly popular in Bangladesh. His Awami League won nearly 98 per cent of the vote in the 1973 elections. However throughout that year and the following one the law and order situation got worse. Political assassinations reached new levels. Mujib felt that the country relied on himself as leader. 'My factories are working, my jute mills, my industries, my cultivators are working. I am in the Asian Development Bank, I am in the Islamic Bank, I am in the Commonwealth,' he said in a 1974 interview with the *Washington Post*.

In January 1975 Sheikh Mujib abolished all political parties and replaced them with a new single national party, the Krishak Sramik Awami League. He took over as President, put an end to parliamentary democracy and tried to stamp out all opposition to his policies. His aim was to eradicate corruption, control population growth and increase agricultural and industrial production. The one party state, he claimed, was 'only for the cause of national unity'.

Political violence

On 15th August 1975 Sheikh Mujib, his wife and some of his family were murdered when gunmen burst into their house. The plot was the work of a small group of middle-ranking army officers. The army declared martial law and banned all political parties. However, power struggles within the army meant this was a time of confusion. Presidents K. M. Ahmed and A. M. Sayem came and went. In April 1977 Major General Ziaur Rahman emerged as the military strong man and became President. Martial law was ended in 1979 but President Ziaur Rahman was himself murdered by a group of army officers in 1981. President Sattar was in power for a few months before yet another military coup brought to power Lieutenant-General Hossain Ershad, who took over as President in December 1983. Parliament was suspended but in 1985 President Ershad won a vote of confidence in his rule. This vote was disputed by his opponents and early in 1986 he formed a new political party, the National Party, with himself as leader.

These rapid political changes have done little to make it possible for Bangladesh to cope with her problems. The huge foreign aid programmes have helped but they can be only a short-term answer. In some ways the large amount of cash coming into the country as aid makes some problems worse. The temptation for some officials to take their own share of this money has led to greater divisions in society. The vast majority remain amongst the poorest in the world but in the smart residential part of Dacca there are some very large and very expensive houses.

17

Agriculture, industry and the growth of population

India

Agriculture has always been the chief activity of India. Nearly three-quarters of the population depend on the land for their living. In the first twenty years after Independence shortage of food was a constant problem. In some years, India had to import around one-tenth of all her grain and even that could not prevent outbreaks of famine. In addition to improving their production to replace imports, Indian farmers need to grow 2 per cent more food each year to match the rise in population. In the twenty years from the late 1960s to the late 1980s India's farmers produced an average of 9 per cent more each year, enough to cope with rising numbers and to cut out most imports of food. There was an especially big increase in the production of food-grains – rice, wheat and maize – which doubled since the early 1960s.

The Green Revolution

A lot of the increase resulted from the 'Green Revolution'. Scientists used their understanding of plant genetics to develop new varieties. The idea was to breed plants bearing more food-grains which were also better at resisting diseases. This is still important work. Superplants are not enough in themselves. Irrigation to provide water and the use of fertilisers are also needed. The developing of irrigation systems and the much wider use of fertilisers have been a feature of India's success in farming.

Food-grains are grown most successfully in the Ganges valley and in Punjab, which supplies 60 per cent of all the grain eaten in India. Crops such as tea in Assam and coffee in the south are exported all over the world and help India's balance of payments. Livestock are an obvious part of Indian village life with as many as 200 million cattle. Forestry and fishing are also important.

Many farmers have very little land. Very few are lucky enough to farm in areas like the Ludhiana district of Punjab, where extensive irrigation produces India's highest yield per acre for rice and wheat. Far more people have no land at all and work as labourers. Despite the improvements of the last decades, life in rural India remains hard.

Industry

Gandhi's struggle against British rule for political independence meant reviving Indians' pride and confidence in their traditional ways of life. This led him to stress the central importance of the people of village India and the need to help their handicraft industries such as spinning and weaving recover from the effects of competition from cheap British factory-made textiles.

Many other Congress leaders had a different vision of India's future. They wanted her to develop modern industries based on European science and technology. Some were in favour of encouraging this through private enterprise but Nehru and his close supporters wanted a planned economy in which the government managed the major industries. When Congress came to power in 1947, Nehru's government gave industrial development a high priority. It divided the economy into two sectors. The government controlled heavy industries and supplies of raw material, while light industries and service businesses were left in private ownership. A Planning Commission was set up, headed by Nehru himself, to control new developments so that the various parts of the economy were kept in balance. It gave guidelines in a series of Five Year Plans, starting with the first which ran from 1951 to 1956.

Steel

By the time of the sixth Five Year Plan (1980–85), one of the most successful developments had been steel. India's first blast furnaces for steel making were lit in 1911 by the Tata Iron and Steel Company. Within twenty years Tata was producing half a million tons of rolled steel a year. After Independence the Tata grew into a huge multinational corporation but state-owned competitors were set up, usually with financial help from overseas. By the mid-1980s India was producing over 10 million tons. She has also created an important chemical industry, vital for supplying fertiliser to farmers as well as maintaining the cotton industry in Gujarat which, like steel, had first developed under Indian management before 1947.

As time went on, many Congress leaders regretted the support they had given to nationalised industries in the early years after Independence, so most of the leading developments in the 1970s and 1980s were carried out by private companies. However, the government still owned the railways, air transport, the armaments industry and the atomic energy plants. Through the India Oil Corporation it also owned the largest share of oil production and sales.

Oil

Oil is just one of India's store of raw materials for industry. She has about a quarter of the world's reserves of iron ore. Her most valuable deposit is coal which is mined in Bihar, West Bengal and Madhya Pradesh but she also has minerals which are vital to new industries. In the 1980s India was producing about four-fifths of the world's mica

The heart of India's steel industry, the Tata steelworks at Jamshedpur.

and was expanding her output of petroleum, natural gas and nuclear energy.

In the 1980s industry made an important contribution to the country's economy but its effects on employment were relatively small. About 7 million people worked in small industries and a similar number in large-scale manufacturing. Such figures needed to be set against the overall size of India's population. In the late 1980s it was at least 750 million, second in the world only to China. Indians made up one in seven of all the people on earth and each year the number increased by no fewer than 15 million.

Population growth

Nehru's government gave high priority from the start to trying to control this growth in population. A poster and leaflet campaign was launched to persuade people to have fewer children. Families with just one or two children were given some tax benefits. This campaign has continued off and on ever since, but with little success. In the decade of the 1960s India's population increased by no less than twenty-five per cent.

In the mid 1970s, Sanjay Gandhi, the son of Prime Minister Indira Gandhi, was accused of pushing the population control campaign so hard that harsh and unacceptable methods were used by local officials. Stories leaked out to the foreign press of the forced sterilisation of

Pilgrims bathing in the Ganges at the sacred Hindu city of Varanasi (formerly Benares) in the mid 1970s. The left-bank of the river is lined with flights of steps like these, called ghats, where pilgrims bathe in order to have their sins washed away. It is the ambition of every devout Hindu to be cremated here when they die and to have their ashes scattered on the waters of the Ganges. The signs on the umbrellas are government family-planning slogans.

people in villages. 'They demanded a *lakh* (10,000) of rupees or twenty-five cases for sterilisation and when I was unable to give them either, our house was pulled down,' Rukaya Begum, a widow with eight children, told Indian journalists in May 1977.

Pakistan

Agriculture

Pakistan is a fortunate country as far as food production is concerned. Crops can be grown on just a third of the land area but this gives enough wheat, rice and sugar to feed the population and more. Rice is Pakistan's most valuable export, mainly to other Islamic countries. Fruits and dates are grown in the mountainous west but the power-house of agriculture is the fertile plain watered by the five rivers. The state of the irrigation system based on these rivers is literally a matter of life and death for Pakistan. The division of Punjab between Pakistan and India in 1947 seemed to threaten this supply of water and created tensions that still exist today.

Half the workforce of Pakistan work on the land. There are some 4 million farms, but nine out of ten of them are very small, less than twenty-five acres. At the time of Partition in 1947 there were some very large private estates as well. Zulfikar Ali Bhutto was himself from a rich landowning family in Sind Province, but when he came to power at the end of 1971 he was determined to take action against the private landlords.

Land reform

By 1977 he had taken nearly 3½ million acres from private landlords and handed much of it to tenant farmers. A law of January 1977 limited landowners to 100 irrigated or 200 non-irrigated acres. The great majority of smaller farmers were to pay no tax. Only a short while later, Bhutto and his radical Pakistan People's Party were driven from power by the army (see page 100).

General Zia did not continue Bhutto's radical land policy. However, the changes stood and by the late 1980s agricultural production in Pakistan was growing at around ten per cent a year. The irrigation system was still being developed with some big projects but it proved difficult in Pakistan as in other new countries to help the tenant farmers take up new methods of crop growing. Just a quarter of the population could read or write, despite increased government spending on education, including a campaign for adult literacy and more teachers in schools. Primary education in Pakistan is free and compulsory but in the later 1980s less than one child in two actually attended a primary school. Farmers who cannot read find it difficult to follow new ideas about planting methods, new varieties of crops and fertiliser, or the use of new tools.

Cotton

Cotton is by far Pakistan's most important non-food crop. Some of the huge crop is exported as raw cotton but more goes directly into the cotton mills to be made into thread and cloth. The textile industry is the biggest in Pakistan. The cotton mills are still privately owned but most other large employers are in the publicly owned industries.

Other industries

In 1947 there was little industrial development in Pakistan. Apart from textiles and sugar there was no sign that private companies would grow without government help. Successive governments of Pakistan have tried in their different ways to give industry a boost. Bhutto was most keen on the state-owned sector. In 1972 he re-organised the public sector companies under a Board of Industrial Management. Since 1977 there has been much more help for private, especially small, industries but the public sector has grown too. In 1983 steel production began at the Pakistan Steel mill at Port Qasim near Karachi. A large joint project with Saudi Arabia for aluminium processing was approved in 1981.

Despite an eight per cent growth rate in manufacturing, not enough money has yet been invested in industry to keep Pakistan competitive in the world market. The world demand for textiles has been uncertain and the aggressive newcomers in Asia like South Korea and Taiwan are developing fast.

Energy

The Indus and its five tributary rivers generate over half the electricity needs of Pakistan. The huge Tarbela Dam on the Indus is the biggest project. The Indus Water Treaty of 1960 between Pakistan and India is the basis of a large-scale canal building scheme in the Indus basin. The other main source of energy is natural gas, piped into the big cities from western Pakistan for domestic and industrial use. There is also some coal, oil and iron ore.

Population

In many ways Pakistan is well placed to take advantage of her natural resources, but only if the growth in her population can be slowed down. By the year 2000 there will be over 150 million with over half in the cities.

A crowded street in the main bazaar (shopping centre) of Rawalpindi. The building in the background is a cinema: films are an important part of the modern culture of Pakistan, India and Bangladesh.

Bangladesh

The three most important things in the agriculture of Bangladesh are rice, jute and water. The country has too little rice, too much jute and either too little or too much water.

Grains

Bangladesh has always been an agricultural region. Rice has been grown in this fertile delta from earliest times. It remains by far the most important food crop, providing more than 85 per cent of calories in the average diet. During the years when the area was part of Pakistan (1947–1971), the production of rice grew by 2½ per cent but the population rose by 3 per cent. People ate less but rice had to be imported, over a million tons a year from the mid 1960s. Since Independence in 1971 these imports have doubled but the problem has got worse. The last decade has seen an increase in population from 80 to 100 million but rice production has only gone up from 12 to 14½ million tons. The mathematics of hunger are all too easy to do.

Jute

Jute is a plant which produces tough fibres used in ropes of all sorts. Bangladesh produces about 70 per cent of the world's jute supply. This tough plant is the country's only export earner but it faces competition from other jute producers and from synthetic fibres. Jute plantations were first opened in the nineteenth century almost entirely by planters from the east coast of Scotland where jute processing was an important industry. Since then it has had its ups and downs. When the world price for jute falls, the economy of Bangladesh suffers badly. Many developing countries rely very heavily on one or two commodity crops in this way, but Bangladesh is in a weaker position than most.

Water control

Three-quarters of all journeys in Bangladesh are by water. The network of rivers and canals keeps the land fertile and, with the sea, provides fish. In the dry season, areas without irrigation suffer from water shortage. If the monsoon rains fail there is widespread starvation. This happened in 1972.

A more common problem is flooding. Then the great rivers of Bangladesh burst their banks, sweeping away all but the most massive flood defences. One of the reasons for the amount of water entering the rivers was that many square miles of forest had been cut for timber and not replanted with trees which would have taken up much of the moisture in the soil.

From June until September the south-west monsoon winds bring the rains from over the Bay of Bengal. At the start there is a quick drop in temperature, with strong winds and lashing rain. Five or six times a year these winds reach cyclone force. The heavier cyclones are national disasters, with winds over 100 mph. The worst in recent times was in November 1970, followed by a huge tidal wave the day after. The coastal areas suffered most but the whole country was damaged. An estimated 30,000 people died. In the following year man continued the work of nature. The civil war which began at the end of 1971 caused

Flooding in north Bangladesh in 1975.

great damage to crops, irrigation systems and property. Millions were killed, wounded or fled their homes.

Industries

The birth of Bangladesh cut the links with West Pakistan (see Chapter 15). The protected market for such things as tea, matches and paper was lost. Sheikh Mujib Rahman's government took over the numerous jute mills abandoned by their West Pakistani owners. All jute mills were nationalised and so were sugar and large cotton mills.

The ten corporations set up to run these industries suffered from inexperienced management. There were more problems with the erratic supply of electricity, unreliable transport and a shortage of raw materials. Production fell, factories and mills closed and unemployment climbed steeply. By early 1975, industrial unrest was one main reason for the government taking emergency powers.

Textiles

In 1982 the military government led by General Ershad made a change in industrial policy one of its first acts. Jute and textiles were de-nationalised and returned to private owners. In fact the largest area of industry in the country was small-scale cottage industry which had remained in many private hands. Some 1½ million people worked in these cottage industries, mainly making textiles on handlooms as well as carpets. Today the goods made by these handworkers have only a small place in world sales. Two centuries ago the fine muslin, silk and brocade of the area were shipped all over Asia and Europe where they were in great demand for making into the most fashionable and expensive dresses. This important and profitable eighteenth-century trade was ruined by the coming of cheap machine-made textiles in the British Industrial Revolution.

Bangladesh, in the late 1980s, is just about the poorest and most overpopulated country on earth. Its main resource, the great system of rivers which bring rich silt down to the delta and provide a complete communications network, is also its greatest hazard.

The Ganges

There are large quantities of fish in the rivers and in the sea. These are an important source of food. Apart from natural gas, Bangladesh has few natural resources. Arguments over the use of the waters of the Ganges have put a strain on the friendly relations with India since 1971. In 1974 India completed the building of the Farraka Barrage, a great dam on the Ganges only twelve miles from the border with Bangladesh. India wanted to divert water down the Hooghly River to flush out the silted-up port of Calcutta. A decade of negotiations has not yet solved these and other arguments about water use between Bangladesh and India.

Despite its great difficulties, Bangladesh is rich in culture and tradition. There is a much clearer understanding now than in the 1950s that population control can only be effective when taken together with improved living standards, jobs and literacy. These were the main aims of the 1980–85 development plan. They offered some hope for the future.

18
Migration

'Migration' is the word used to describe movement of people away from their homes. They may move to the next village, the nearest town, to the other end of the country, or half-way round the world. 'Emigration' occurs when people leave their own country to settle permanently in another. The decision to move in a family group is not an easy one to take. It means a great upheaval and an uncertain future. Over the centuries migrants have had many reasons for moving. Hunger or fear for their lives or to find work and better chances for their families – one or more of these reasons are usually behind the decision to go. Migrants may plan their move with care or flee without notice or possessions. Since 1947 South Asia has seen many millions on the move in both ways and for all these reasons.

India

In 1947 Partition tore communities apart in Punjab in the north-west and Bengal in the north-east. At times like these, nobody can make a careful head count. Terrified crowds of refugees do not stand in queues. The best estimate is that some 5½ million refugees crossed the new border in Punjab each way.

Refugees

Another huge exchange of population took place in Bengal in the north-east. Well over a million Hindus left East Bengal, moving west into India. A similar number of Muslims, mainly from Bihar, began moving east into East Bengal after the communal massacres of November 1946.

There are perhaps 15 million refugee stories to tell from South Asia in 1947. All begin in chaos but some have happy endings because of the enterprise and talent of families in their new homes.

Country-town migrants

Slower, but no less dramatic, has been migration into the cities by country people looking for work. 300 families a day arrive in Bombay,

India's second largest city after Calcutta. A third of India's cloth is made in Bombay's textile mills and many migrants come looking for work in them. Working conditions are poor but the pay is quite good by standards in the area.

Bombay, a busy trading city and the centre of a huge Indian film industry, used to pride itself on the quality of its city life. In the late 1970s the increasingly crowded city began to spill over on to the pavements. The city authorities, worried about rising street crime and the spread of disease, decided to destroy these pavement villages in 1982. Bulldozers flattened the wood, cardboard and string shacks but the pavement people won a court case to stop the destruction of their homes.

Bombay is still growing fast, spreading to the east and north. In the 1990s nearly 10 million people live there. It is expected to be 16 million by the year 2000. No wonder the celluloid dreams made in Bombay's film studios are so popular.

Migrants can be unwelcome in the communities they join, especially if they are successful. South of Bombay is the state of Karnataka where most of India's coffee is grown. During the 1940s a steady stream of migrants, many of them Muslims, arrived in the coffee district from the next-door state of Kerala. Today some 40 per cent of the population of this district is from Kerala, and they own most of the coffee plantations. The local people resent the success of these Kerala migrants. There have been ugly clashes and angry marches.

The Gulf

In the last decade there has been a large increase in the number of Indians going as migrant workers to Saudi Arabia and other states in the Gulf. Bahrain drilled its first successful oil well in 1932 and opened a recruiting office in Bombay four years later. After the war Kuwait and Saudi Arabia began to need migrant workers as well to support the rapid growth in their oil-related economies. However, it was the oil price explosion of 1973–4 which triggered off a tidal wave of labour migration to the Gulf States. By the early 1980s there were some 6 million migrant workers in the Gulf, a hundred-fold increase on the 1970 figure.

Nearly a million of these migrant workers are from India, young men mainly from rural areas. They work in construction, in public services and as domestic servants. There is a wide range from skilled to unskilled but all earn perhaps five or six times more than they could at home. These million migrant workers in the Gulf are a small proportion of India's over 200 million workers, but between them in 1981 they sent home a staggering £1,000 million in remittances, a quarter of India's total export earnings.

Between 1981 and 1983 the value of oil exports from the Gulf dropped by a half and it seemed that the demand for migrant workers would fall. Certainly migrants had to accept rather lower wages and poorer conditions. On the other hand, the Indian government negotiated with the oil producing states to set minimum standards for migrant workers.

There is nothing new in this migration of Indian labour. It was the system of indentured labour which brought a large Indian community to South Africa, where Gandhi's political life began. In the Caribbean, both Guyana and Trinidad have a substantial population of Indian origin who are descended from indentured labourers taken there in the nineteenth century. The same is true of other countries – Mauritius and Malaysia, for example.

Pakistan

Large-scale movements

The resettlement of more than 5 million Muslim migrants from northern India was one of the first major tasks of the new state of Pakistan in 1947. On a smaller scale, migration across frontiers had long been part of the lives of some large tribal groups in the north-west corner of British India. Some 4 million Baluchis live in Pakistan's western province. Another million live across the border in Iran and Afghanistan. As industry has spread west into the area it has brought in workers from other parts of the country. At the same time a steady number of Baluchis has left the area, migrating to the industrial areas of Pakistan, especially to Karachi. Baluchi migrants have also moved west into Iran and farther on to the Gulf. Migration of this sort within Pakistan is the main reason for the growth in size of the main cities. Both Karachi, the main sea port, and Lahore, capital of Punjab Province, have doubled their populations in the last decade.

Pakistan's other main ethnic group has also been on the move since 1947. 12 million Pathans live in the country and are the major group in the North-West Frontier Province (NWFP). Pathans are also the largest group in Afghanistan to the north. In the last twenty years Pathans have migrated in large numbers to industrial centres looking for work, usually unskilled jobs. There are said to be a million Pathans in and around Karachi. However, their home, North West Frontier Province, has increased its population despite the migrations. The main reason is the flood of refugees from Afghanistan. In December 1979 regular troops of the USSR invaded Afghanistan. Refugees from the fighting in Afghanistan's eastern provinces began to cross into Pakistan in large numbers. By the end of 1980, 40,000 to 50,000 were arriving each month. There are now some 2½ million refugees, few of whom are likely ever to return to Afghanistan. Most are settling in NWFP.

Afghanistan

Despite support from the International Red Cross and other agencies, the strain on Pakistan's resources was enormous. One opposition leader said that the government was turning Pakistan into a *Mohajristan*, a land of immigrants, and demanded that the refugees be sent back. The refugees were a security risk as well as an economic burden as the government of Pakistan could not effectively police the long border or control the highland tribes on both sides of the frontier. Afghan resistance fighters operated openly in the refugee camps. In 1989 the USSR

An Afghan family pause for a rest in the snow in the mountains along the Afghan–Pakistan border in 1981. Many such Afghan refugees gathered in camps near Peshawar in northern Pakistan.

withdrew her forces from Afghanistan. This ended the risk that Pakistan would be faced with retaliation from the USSR for the activities of freedom fighters who had sheltered in the refugee camps. However, many of them continued to take part in a civil war which was partly between the Afghan government in Kabul and the freedom fighters, partly a struggle for leadership between the various anti-government groups. The new government of Benazir Bhutto tried to remain neutral but while the fighting went on it was still faced with the problem of large numbers of refugees who were often linked to one or other of the guerilla armies in Afghanistan.

Like India, Pakistan has supplied many migrant workers to the Gulf States. In the 1980s there were 2 million of them who sent home more money each year than Pakistan earned from her entire export effort. The government well knew the value to the country of these migrant workers. Pakistan offered them tax exemption and a welfare programme including low-cost insurance, legal aid, social welfare, health, housing and education benefits. Any decline in the need for migrant workers in the Gulf States will hit the economy of Pakistan hard.

Bangladesh

During the civil war in 1971, 10 million people crossed the border into India from East Bengal. This huge movement of people was only a short-term migration. Most returned to Bangladesh after the fighting ended, though to the cities rather than the countryside from where most had come. Somehow the Indian authorities coped with this invasion at the same time as they gave military support to the Bangladesh freedom fighters, the Mukti Bahini.

The results of war

The migrants returned to a country full of hope but faced with awesome problems. One of these could only be solved by shifting large numbers of people between India, Pakistan and Bangladesh. About 90,000 West Pakistanis, mainly soldiers, had surrendered to the Indian army at the end of the civil war. Many thousands of Bengalis had been arrested by the West Pakistanis and sent back west to prison. Lastly the Biharis, the non-Bengali Muslims who migrated to East Bengal in 1947, felt threatened and persecuted in Bangladesh. They wanted to leave if anyone would have them.

In 1972 the Prime Ministers of India and of Pakistan, Indira Gandhi and Zulfikar Ali Bhutto, met at Simla in India. The ice was broken. Two years later Pakistan formally accepted the existence of Bangladesh and the three countries began to make progress on people shifting. Later that year Bhutto made a state visit to Bangladesh and the United Nations announced that repatriation was complete. Prisoners of war had returned home and over 100,000 Biharis had been accepted by Pakistan.

In fact over half a million Biharis applied to leave Bangladesh and go to Pakistan. Many remain stranded in large, squalid refugee camps. A doctor working in these camps in 1977 wrote: 'It is difficult to imagine how it can be possible for the Commonwealth nations to allow such monstrosities to continue to exist in a Commonwealth country.' In 1981 the British MP David Ennals revisited one of the camps:

> 'The same camp, Muhammadpur, no more than five miles from the centre of Dacca is still a sea of mud and excrement, an open sewer surrounding broken-down shacks with corrugated iron roofs, housing tens of thousands of desperate people waiting, still waiting, to go to the country of their choice.'

Bangladesh has a slice of the Gulf migrant labour market, where skilled workers can earn between six and eight times as much as at home. The cash sent home by the 100,000 Bangladeshis in the Gulf was a very welcome source of foreign exchange.

In the mid-1980s Bangladeshi migrants became a major issue in the Indian state of Assam. Migrants, many illegal, were attracted by the prospects of work on Assam's many tea plantations. A political party, the Assam Peoples' Front, was formed to campaign against the increase in Bangladeshi migrants. This party won a landslide victory in the 1985 elections. India's central government then considered building a boundary fence along the border with Bangladesh to prevent illegal immigration in the future.

Migration to Britain

In the 1950s Britain was short of workers in many branches of industry and in services such as transport and health. Workers were recruited from India and Pakistan just as they were from the Caribbean. Migrants from Pakistan and India who settled in Britain were entitled to UK citizenship because they came from a Commonwealth country.

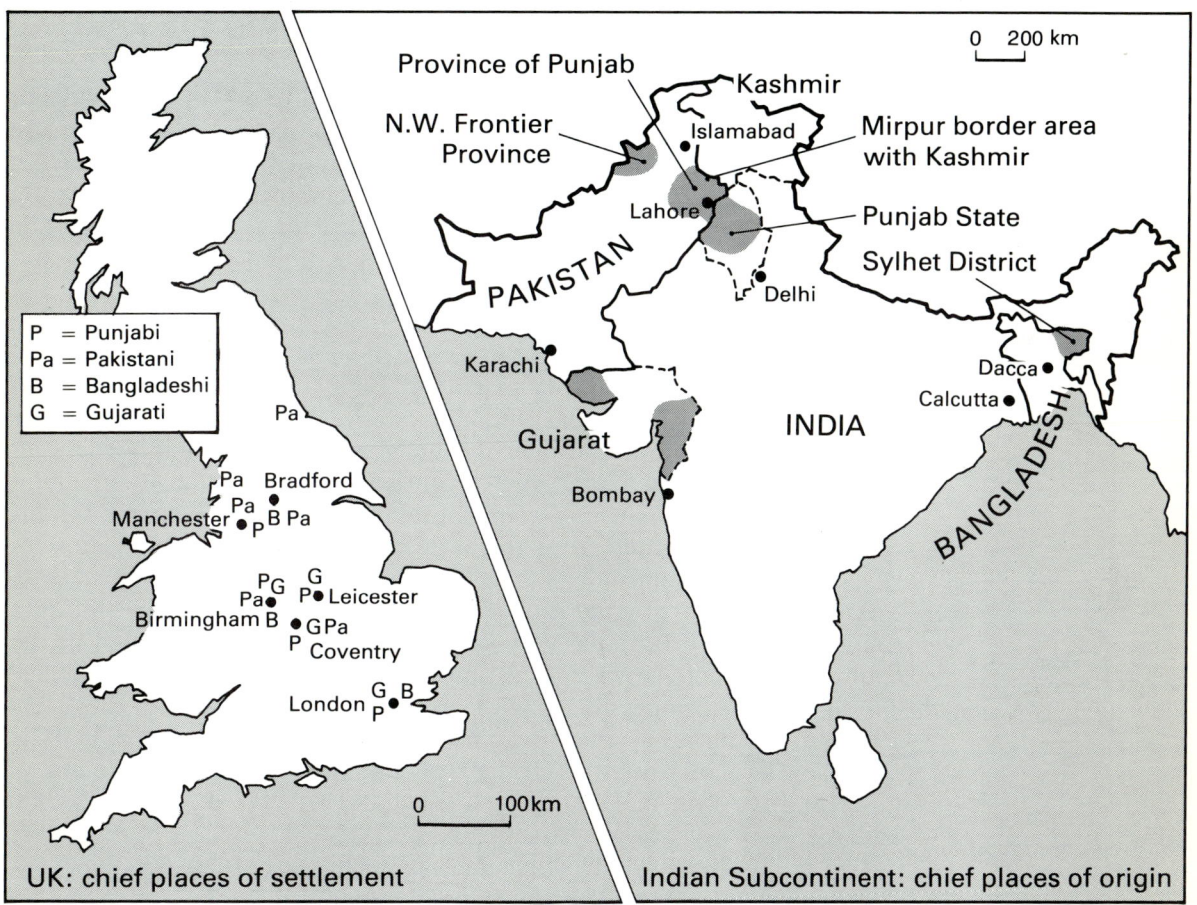

P = Punjabi
Pa = Pakistani
B = Bangladeshi
G = Gujarati

UK: chief places of settlement

Indian Subcontinent: chief places of origin

Emigration from the subcontinent to the UK.

Commonwealth citizens

By 1955 there were 55,000 Indian and Pakistani people who had entered Britain since the Second World War. Until the end of the 1950s between 7,000 and 8,000 continued to go to Britain each year. Most were still male workers but a growing number were wives and children joining husbands and fathers who had travelled earlier and spent several hard years earning enough to provide a home as well as sending money back to their families in India and Pakistan.

In 1962 the number of Indian and Pakistani people in Britain was still small and nearly all were doing the hardest jobs on the most unpopular shifts and living in the poorest of Britain's inner-city housing. These disadvantages did not stop anti-immigrant feelings. In 1962 the Commonwealth Immigration Act restricted entry into Britain from Commonwealth countries to those who held employment vouchers issued before they arrived. The law had a much greater effect on potential immigrants from India, Pakistan and the Caribbean than it did on potential immigrants from the old 'white' Dominions such as Australia. More than 90,000 South Asian people entered Britain in the eighteen months before the voucher system started. After that the number of immigrants began to fall but there was now a larger number of people in India, Pakistan and later Bangladesh waiting to come to Britain.

In 1971 a second Commonwealth Immigration Act was passed. After it became law in 1973, no more employment vouchers were issued and the only people allowed into Britain from India, Pakistan and Bangladesh were the relatives and dependants of settlers already there. Many of these found it extremely difficult to pass through the many checks at British consular offices in the Indian sub-continent and at the airports in Britain.

Homelands

Most of the migrants to Britain moved from a few regions in the three countries. The majority of British Bangladeshi families are from the Sylhet district in the east of Bangladesh. British Pakistanis mostly came from Punjab State, especially the Mirpur area, which borders on Kashmir, or from the North-West Frontier Province. Gujarati-speaking British Indians came from Gujarat State in Western India and Punjabi-speaking Indians came from the state of Punjab and include most of Britain's Sikh population.

Another group of migrants to Britain arrived by a more indirect route. They were Indians, very often from Gujarat, who settled in the countries of East Africa at the time when they were British colonies. These became independent with African majority rule in the early 1960s. In some areas there was hostility towards Indian people. The most severe harassment of Indian people was by the government of General Idi Amin in Uganda in 1971 and 1972. He drove out 80,000 Indians, many of whom settled in Britain.

In 1976 it was estimated that there were altogether 390,000 people of Indian and 246,000 of Pakistani and Bangladeshi origin in Britain. By the later 1980s the total number was nearer three-quarters of a million but well over half were children and adults who had been born in Britain. Many lived in widely spread districts throughout the country but the greatest number still made their homes in the towns where the first migrants had settled.

It was still true that industries and services depended on their work but it was also true that they suffered the highest levels of unemployment during the recession of the 1980s. Those who held on to jobs often suffered discrimination over promotion just as they did over housing.

In some communities the settlers were the victims of harassment including damage to their houses and physical attacks on themselves.

Race relations

The British government first attempted to deal with the racial discrimination through the Race Relations Act of 1965 which made it illegal to discriminate against people of any race in a public place. It set up a Race Relations Board to investigate complaints about such discrimination but this had little real effect. In 1968 another Act made discrimination illegal in key areas of life such as education, housing and employment. Employers, landlords, housing managers and others with influence in these key areas showed little sign of respecting the law or the reasons for it. In 1976 the Racial Equality Act tried to deal with this, as well as making it clear that anyone trying to stir up racial hatred in action, speech or writing was breaking the law. A Commission for Racial Equality was set up to investigate examples of discrimination. In some areas its work led to improvements but by the end of the 1980s there was still a lot of evidence that people from India, Pakistan and Bangladesh, along with other ethnic minorities in Britain, were at a disadvantage in housing, education and employment, and that the more ugly forms of harassment had not ended.

INDEX

ACKNOWLEDGEMENTS

We are grateful to the following for permission to reproduce photographs: British in India Museum, page 3; British Library, pages 13, 14, 23, 27, 30, 36, 46, 68; Douglas Dickins, pages 81, 87, 96, 100, 106, 108; Hulton-Deutsch Collection, pages 34, 40, 43, 48, 56, 70, 71, 74, 76, 94, 105; National Museum of Photography, Film & Television, page 5; Nehru Memorial Museum, Delhi, page 54; Frank Spooner Pictures, page 110; Topham Picture Library, pages 60, 115.
We are unable to trace the copyright holder of the following and would be grateful for any information that would enable us to do so, page 19.

Cover: Nehru and Jinnah meeting together at Yarrows in Simla. Photo: Popperfoto.

Short extracts in this book were taken from: page 12, Syed Ahmed Khan in a letter to Mawlawi Tasadduq, in *Sir Syed ke chand nadir khutut*; page 25, Edwin S Montagu, *An Indian Diary*, London, 1931; page 26, Jawaharlal Nehru, *The Discovery of India*, The Signet Press, Calcutta, 1945; page 47, Devadas Gandhi to Jawaharlal Nehru, Nehru Papers, NNML; page 51, J Nehru, *An Autobiography*, The Bodley Head; page 52, *Important Speeches of Jawaharal Nehru*, Presidential Address, 1936; Subhas Chandra Bose, *Netaji Speaks to the Nation*; page 53, M K Gandhi to Agatha Harrison, April 30 1936, Home Political, File No. 32/4/36, NAI; page 54, M K Akbar, *Nehru: The Making of India*, Viking, 1988; page 55, S S Pirzada (ed), *The Foundations of Pakistan* Vol 2; page 56 ibid; page 60, M J Akbar, *op cit*; D G Tendulkar, *Mahatma*, Bombay, 1951-4; page 62, Slim, *Defeat into Victory*, Cassell, 1956; page 66, Jamil-ud-Din Ahmad, *Speeches and Writings of Mr Jinnah* Vol II, Lahore, 1947; page 70, A Campbell-Johnson, *Mission with Mountbatten*, Robert Hale Ltd, 1951; page 71, M J Akbar, *op cit*; page 74, Louis Fischer, *The Life of Mahatma Gandhi*, Harper and Row, 1950; page 85, Jamil-ud-Din Ahmad, *op cit*; page 116, David Ennals, *The Biharis in Bangladesh*, Minority Rights Group Report II (4th Revised), 1982.

We are indebted to the Sri Aurobindo Ashram Trust for permission to reproduce Sri Aurobindo Ghose's translation of the Bengali poem 'Bande Mataram' by Bankim Chandra Chatterji from *Collected Poems and Plays*, *Volume II* by Aurobindo Ghose (Pondicherry, India, 1942).